INTERLUDES WITH Nature

CAROLYNN F McCULLY

Primix Publishing
485c US Highway 1 South
Suite 100
Iselin, NJ 08830
www.primixpublishing.com
Phone: 1-800-538-5788

© 2024 Carolynn F McCully. All rights reserved.

No part of this book may be reproduced, stored in a retrieval system, or transmitted by any means without the written permission of the author.

Published by Primix Publishing: 08/20/2024

ISBN: 979-8-89194-237-0(sc)
ISBN: 979-8-89194-238-7(e)

Library of Congress Control Number: 2024911947

Any people depicted in stock imagery provided by iStock are models, and such images are being used for illustrative purposes only.

Certain stock imagery © iStock.

Because of the dynamic nature of the Internet, any web addresses or links contained in this book may have changed since publication and may no longer be valid. The views expressed in this work are solely those of the author and do not necessarily reflect the views of the publisher, and the publisher hereby disclaims any responsibility for them.

CONTENTS

Prelude xi
Author's Note xiii
Waters Edge Gift. xv

NATURES CALL FOR COMMUNICATION

Buzzing Agreement. 1
Enchanting Visitor 9
A Squirrely Bargain 18
Feathered Charmer. 28
    Joyfilled Intentions 29
    Chance Meeting on The Hill 33
    Sweet and Lucky Moment 36
    Distinctive Farewell 40
A Sweet Sharing Moment 45

CHALLENGING INTERLUDES

The Perception Of Giants. 55
    A Child's View 56
    Two Facets of Becoming A Giant 61
    Giant in Mind or Deed. 65

GOING WITH THE FLOW

Feeling the Energy Flow 71
Swimming Pool Wonders 73
Lost in the Waves 77
Rough Ride in Rapids. 81

RELAXING IN NATURE

Memorable Moments 89
Chipmunk Saftey Trail 94
Wilderness Wonder. 97
A Walk with Nature 105

SURPRISING NATURE CONNECTIONS

Emotional Weather Link. 109
A Nature Walk Interruption 113
Unexpected Encounter 116
The Allure of Nature 123
Good Deeds Gone Astray. 127
Monkey Misadventure 134
A Startling Notion 140

HEALING POWER OF NATURE

Restoring Energy 149
Finding A Way 158
A Cardinal's Call 162
Conclusion 169

"There is a way that nature speaks, that land speaks.

Most of the time, we are not patient enough, or

quiet enough to pay attention to the story."

-Linda Hogan

This book is dedicated to my daughter Cara, 1965 – 2023. Cara inspired me to search for evidence for the unexplainable and a most ardent desire to put what I find into to words. A seed of curiosity about unusual interconnections between nature and us as humans was planted after a most peculiar incident that took place when she was around four years old. It was very early in the morning when she came running into my bedroom all excited and out of breath, exclaiming, "Mommy, there are bears loose! Will they come here?" Of course, my first thought was that she had a nightmare, and I tried my best to reassure her that no such thing could happen. It must have been a dream. Her little body shook with excitement, so much so that I mistook it as anxiety and fear as she tried to continue to convince me with her story. My explanation did nothing to pacify her resolve that three bears were loose in the city and might be lost. I spent some time trying to settle her down before taking her back to her bed, reassuring her that there were no bears in the city and that since we live on the 8th floor of an apartment building, it would not be possible even if such a thing were to be true. They would not be visiting us! Before she settled back to sleep, she looked up with such a knowing and beautiful smile declaring softly, , "That's okay, Mommy, they are still out there."

If you could only imagine my surprise later that same morning! While listening to the radio, an announcement came that three bears had escaped from the Toronto Zoo during the night and were loose in the city streets. By early morning they were unharmed, captured and returned. Not surprisingly I was left in wonderment and awe to ponder on the interconnection possibilities between all the facets of nature's species. To this day, this experience continues to perplex my mind giving me pause to think there is more to this life than what meets the eye.

PRELUDE

"When we speak of privilege, we talk about a right possessed by an individual or a group. So, the following has been compiled as an anthology of proof that humans can connect with all life forms if we are open to it."

For whatever reason, Mother Nature has assigned privilege to certain people to communicate with nature's beings. The prerequisite for this privilege is to be open and willing to communicate with nature's creatures in whatever manner presents itself."

Imagine a moment of pure connection, a moment when you realize that communication with life forms other than ourselves is not only possible, but natural. This is the essence of our inherent connection with nature.

"With that being said, enjoy reading these touching and sometimes funny stories of human-animal and environmental interaction that cannot be denied as proof of two-way communication between man and various living species."

- Glenys Acorn

AUTHOR'S NOTE

A purposeful connection with nature unquestionably provides the means to expand our understanding as we interact with various facets of the magical world we share with all energies found on this planet. It cannot be denied that every intended search, successful or not, brings fascinating learning, and with little effort, nature can move us to a place of wonder and awe, continually surprising us as we ponder *'unexpected'* interconnection moments that present themselves. Ready or not, we are surrounded by nature in all its forms, providing untold opportunities to recognize that nature is a most outstanding teacher while dealing with life's challenges. It would seem that having once experienced an interlude with any aspect of this world of nature gives one pause to reflect on the wisdom gained from such an encounter becoming part of one's learning journey. It matters not the nature of the experience; the desire to express what has occurred would most assuredly be enjoyable for those willing to listen and explore what can be gained in the exchange. Such are the stories you will find throughout these pages, filled with unique interludes with nature expressed through many grateful heart and mind experiences waiting to be heard.

It seems befitting to start with the unusual 'energy' interlude with nature that inspired this author's previous writing, 'Dream Whispers.'

WATERS EDGE GIFT

*"Come forth into the light things;
let nature be your teacher."*

-William Wordsworth

As described in 'Dream Whispers,' the inspiration to share such an unusual interlude began with an invitation to spend time at the other end of the country, bringing appreciation to the phrase, *"Change is as good as a rest."* Unbeknownst to me, a remarkable energy connection was about to occur after finding what could only be labelled *"an extraordinary gift"* that had washed up from the shores of a little lake in the BC mountains while camping with my sisters. During this much-needed break, I became embroiled in a magical call to nature's energy and awe that remains ongoing today! The area provided the perfect backdrop for a much-needed rest from the chaos that seemed to be taking over my life, bringing a whole new meaning to the well-known phrase, 'Nothing beats getting back to Nature.' This experience proved an ideal opportunity to share my thoughts in a wilderness world of nature, where life and tranquillity intertwine in breathtaking beauty.

Settling into this enchanting energy voyage began with a quick trek into the surrounding campsite area, allowing a firsthand glimpse of what makes nature so appealing, whetting one's appetite for all that could be expected over the next few days. Although it took a moment for the peace and serenity of this charming setting to soak in, a quick tour of my surroundings presented an impression of stepping into a small corner of the *'Garden of Eden.'* At this first taste of solitude, I lost myself in a world of nature's alluring charm. An in-depth enticement to connect with nature took such a firm hold on my heart and imagination that I was captivated from that moment on.

Majestic mountains were the backdrop of a splendid view of the peaceful lake surrounding the campsite property. Exploring the lake and surrounding area was high on the list of things to do over the next few sunshine-filled days. Fully immersed in the sights and sounds of nature, one could not help but become spellbound with tantalizing notions of imaginative forest life. Later in the day, it was time for a mid-afternoon stroll on the beachfront after such a stimulating morning hike. While enjoying the slight cooling breeze from the lake, I was drawn to a strange-looking object resting in the pebbles at the water's edge. The item had been pointed out to me by my sister, who felt it would intrigue my curiosity. She could not have been more spot on. Filled with fascination, I thought it natural to follow my intuitive urge to investigate. At first glance, it appeared to be a small piece of driftwood.

Captivated by the unusual shape, small size, and dull-gray coating of the driftwood, I eagerly picked it up for a closer look. It did not matter that it was merely a lifeless piece of wood. I momentarily held it close to my heart as an unusual natural treasure. It was hard to comprehend what happened next after turning it over in my hands to brush off loose bits of dirt and sand. My heart quickened, realizing a strange awareness of a most peculiar faint vibration coming from the driftwood. I gave myself over to this mindful moment and immediately became aware of tuning into an odd energy frequency I had never felt before. At that point, I did not know if the vibration was coming from me or the object in my hand. It was like a wave of energy going back and forth from the object to me and from me to the object as if we were connected. The astonishing moment made me feel this was much more than an old piece of dead wood, and I was captivated by a passing thought, *"Perhaps all life forms hold some undying energy, even this old, weathered piece of driftwood."*

This energy-based notion immediately became the inspirational tone of what was to follow. This little gift from the lake would become a special keepsake, a reminder of a most intriguing connection with nature found throughout the campgrounds, and a treasured lake souvenir from my vacation. On returning to the trailer, the little driftwood was added to a collection of smaller stones gathered during the day's outing and placed on a large rock close to the fire pit. For the rest of the day, I pondered the meaning of such a find and the ever-increasing sense of mystery and intrigue that this piece of wood had evoked in my imagination.

A strange awakening to magical thinking had been triggered, along with an unbounded curiosity about the hidden secrets of nature yet to be discovered. This curiosity and energy-rousing thoughts ran wild and free during what turned out to be a most delightful outing of the day. I decided such an inspirational gift deserved a thorough cleanup, requiring tender care to keep the fragile pieces intact. At the same time, I thought, *"Who can tell? Perhaps this little driftwood treasure has an important and insightful message for me."*

It was hard to see anything but a plea for understanding considering the shape and position of this piece of driftwood resting so gracefully on the rock. How could it be seen in any other way bearing in mind the pose that reminded me of something almost sacred? It seemed to me that those root tentacles and outstretched arms were clasped in a attitude of prayer, begging to be noticed. The overall posture alone gave the impression that this piece of wood had something important to declare and that resisting such a plea for attention was impossible. All that was necessary was for someone to take the time to listen. While entertaining these fanciful thoughts, I began experiencing an oddly strange yet familiar feeling of a door slowly opening.

Later in the evening, before heading down to the campfire, I gathered the necessary tools for a decisive cleaning procedure to ready the piece for the next step, a vital and vigorous sanding. Great care was needed to dig out all the debris collected over time in the driftwood crevices. Astonishment took hold with the depth of hopeful anticipation I felt and for how much attention was required to bring this little driftwood to a thing of beauty. I was about to embark on what could only be described as an urgent quest to discover more about the curious energy of nature. Bound and determined to uncover the mysteries of this little piece of wood, I settled in at the fire pit with sandpaper and a sharp knife close at hand, ready to begin a new and disarming energy discovery journey.

Incredibly, while picking up the driftwood off the nearby rock, I again experienced that tingling sensation I had felt earlier when I held it close to my heart. This time, however, it was a bit stronger than the faint vibration felt at the water's edge during that first moment of contact. Curious, I brought the little piece of driftwood up to my ear, thinking to myself, *"What is it you have to say to me?"* I was astonished by an unexpected response to my query. Much like a faint but unmistakable murmur or distant but clear echo of awareness came in a quiet but precise whisper, "**Open the door of heart and mind.**" "**Explore and enjoy each of life's moments***.*" I could only shake my head in amazement, unsure what it meant. At this point, I began to doubt my reality-based thinking and thought it best to return attention to the cleaning task.

The origin of this beguiling piece of old wood was soon revealed as I smoothed away the rough gray outer shell. A warm, rich colour slowly emerged. This discovery prodded further attentiveness and a determination to continue despite the incessant sanding and energy required to bring out such hidden beauty. Soon, this persistence paid off in the revelation of a breathtaking display of symmetrical graining, showing streaks of pink and red throughout the curves of the wood. How delightful to discover that my little treasure was undoubtedly a tiny root portion of a red cedar tree. Smiling inwardly, I thought, *"I wonder who discovered whom?"* After much sanding and more buffing, I gently set it aside on the picnic table for the night and, in doing so, let out a deep sigh of contentment as I headed toward my sleeping quarters. While preparing for bed after such an exhilarating yet exhausting day, with nothing less than a racing, curiosity-filled mind, I could only speculate on the magical dreams I would be experiencing throughout the night.

Despite little sleep and an early rise, I felt fresh and strangely euphoric while heading down to the fire pit to welcome the sunrise, which, as it turned out, was another mysterious and joy-filled occasion. Arriving at the picnic table, I saw a most surprising spectacle. Seemingly, those first rays of the morning sun gently stroked the little piece of driftwood, intensifying the richness of newly exposed red cedar graining. For one thrilling moment, a surreal glow radiated from this extraordinary treasure. The sight triggered an untold appreciation for the energy force of nature.

A door of awareness had been opened, offering a new path of gratitude for all forms of life connections. Perhaps through this little gift from the lake, an opportunity would arise to fulfil my growing inspiration, providing the means to share this exceptional experience. This unique connection with nature and the little piece of driftwood took root deep in the heart and mind of this author during her search for expression through various interactions with nature throughout her life, including gathering interactive stories of nature from the lives of others. It is hoped that you, dear readers, will get as much pleasure in reading them as it was in having the opportunity to share them in written form.

Story Reflection

One wonders if opening the door to one's heart and mind has the same meaning as being open and receptive to all that may come in this life. Is it even possible to be receptive to everything that happens in life?

Perhaps it depends on one's mindset regarding unusual life experiences, especially when you consider the possibility of all the negative thoughts and emotions that keep us feeling down, making us feel worse if our minds are closed to anything that can move us in another direction. So…, if our thoughts alone keep us in misery, then perhaps we need to be in a mindset where we are ready and willing to allow those thoughts, along with our misery, to dissipate before we can slowly open ourselves up to change.

So often in life, we find that the very thing that shows up unexpectedly is the means for a change of mindset, most assuredly to a heavy heart, offering a glimmer of joy, peace, or healing, even if only for the moment. Once a new awareness takes hold, there can be no turning back. No matter how small the change, it cannot be undone and holds the key for a different viewpoint to take hold. Maybe the real question in our thinking should consider, does life happen **to us**…*or* **for us**?

NATURES CALL FOR COMMUNICATION

"Let nature be your guide, and you'll find that learning becomes

an endless journey of awe and discovery."

- Gabriel Cruz.

BUZZING AGREEMENT

"In all things of nature, there is something of the marvellous."

- Aristotle

Many years ago, I had come away from church entirely enthralled by one of the most exciting sermon talks I had heard for quite some time. A visiting speaker from a rural area of my church district gave the talk, explaining to the congregation a most unusual event while visiting one of his parishioners. His presentation of one of the many wonders and blessings of God's gifts to this world arrived through a most intriguing experience he had with nature. His story began with a fascinating energy connection while heading out to the barn for a quick word with his friend. Two of the farmer's geese joined him as he walked, making his way towards his intended purpose. He noticed that they seemed to be mimicking him, slowing down, speeding up and coming to a complete stop in unison with his movement. He explained his curiosity about what was happening and indicated to the congregation that he started conversing with the geese. His conversation with them morphed into a query to their understanding that we share the same creator understood by us all as the God of all things in our universe.

Unsure of how he could receive any answer, if any were given and not knowing the language of geese, he decided to improvise by requesting that they give him some sign that they understood what he was talking and thinking about. To his total amazement, they provided a honk as a reply. He, of course, could not resist the urge to test his theory out, so he asked if they would honk twice if they understood and were willing to continue the conversation, and to his complete surprise, they did so with two distinct honks coming from each of them. However, he needed clarification about whether what he had just witnessed came from his softspoken words aimed at them or his thoughts about creation, wanting to believe they understood. It seemed that the back-and-forth words followed by specific number of honks as requested continued up until he arrived at his destination. He declared to the congregation that he was satisfied that a connection had been made. Having practiced his sermon on the geese, he stated he was pretty sure it would be acceptable, especially as the geese seemed quite pleased with what he had to say, demonstrated by continuing their honking as they slowly parted ways. The most significant part of the message, at least for me, was the conversation with the geese. I could not get it out of my mind and decided that first opportunity that came my way to commune with nature, I would not hesitate to find out for myself.

Many weeks had passed before the opportunity to check out the validity of such an experience was put to the test. When I least expected, a similar opportunity nicely presented itself. It was an ideal moment to prove, at least to myself once and for all, that experiencing such a connection with nature was indeed possible. At the time, I lived in a townhouse with a kitchen facing the inner court area of all the houses in the complex. A hornet had entered through the sliding door entrance to my kitchen when one of the kids went out to play and left the screen door open. I at first found it most irritating that the screen door was left open and had to deal with a hornet while preparing supper. It was very upsetting at the time, as the pesky little creature was interfering with my food preparations flying closer to me than what I deemed comfortable.

I grabbed the fly swatter, ready for battle, feeling very annoyed with the disruptive situation. At that exact moment of my first swinging attempt, I remembered my self-promising intention to try to commune with nature. A perfect opportunity had just presented itself! What better chance could there be? I proceeded to fulfill my quest by opening the screen door and took my stance in the middle of the kitchen. After a deep breath, I began my oration, thinking benevolence would need to start with me. I had heard somewhere that communication with nature works well if you visualize what you want to happen while talking. It was said that the chance for any communication success is combined with one's voice, vibrational energy, and emotion and that proper understanding comes in pictures. With these facts in mind, including a burst of faith in the outcome, I was determined to put this understanding to the test.

I called out to the little creature and visualized it coming close. To my wonder and total surprise, it flew closer. Having the fly swatter in hand, I then proceeded with my mission to let it know that it did not belong in my space and that there was no chance of it surviving such a battle to live another day; it would have to leave at once. In my mind, I tried to picture two scenarios. The first was of the hornet flying out the door, and the second, finding it squished on the fly swatter. I verbalized my displeasure of having to kill one of God's little creatures, and my choice would be, of course…, for it to take the first offer and fly to safety! I proceeded to request a sign of understanding, and to my utter amazement, the little creature flew closer to me, circled my head three times, no more, no less, and flew out the door. To be clear, no words could describe how I felt other than, *"How, in this world, does it get any better than that?"*

Having now experienced a connection with one of nature's tiny creatures, I found myself bursting at the seams to tell someone. It just so happened that a friend who lived in the same townhouse complex came by for a visit a short time later, and of course, not holding back, I gave her a descriptive account of what had just happened. I am sure she was amused and, to be truthful, thought me a bit delusional at the time. Nevertheless, it felt good to have shared such a unique experience with someone who, at the very least, shared the pleasure I had in telling the incident despite knowing the whole thing was very odd. It mattered not that she did not understand the concept but that she had a good imagination and could visualize the entire incident.

    A couple of weeks passed before another opportunity to put this new skill to the test came up. It was a beautiful sunny day when my friend, with whom I had previously shared my connection adventure, came rushing through the door in desperation, requesting I come quickly to help her friend who had just arrived home from the hospital. Without hesitation, I followed her to see how I could help. I must admit that I was taken aback when, almost at a run towards her friend's unit, she explained that since I could speak to bees, she desperately needed my help. A part of me was flattered that now, of all times, she believed me. However, I was also very skeptical of my powers to be of any help at all. I was about to put myself in quite a dilemma, unsure of how things would turn out, so much so that I almost turned around, not really wanting to put myself to the test. However, due to the panic in her voice, I decided this would be one of those times when I had to place my faith in a higher power, allowing myself to be a conduit for a more significant cause by putting aside my insecurities.

    My friend explained that her friend had just arrived home with her newborn and had put the baby on the couch and went into the next room to give her husband a list of things to get at the store. As she went to return to her baby in the living room, she became aware of what, in her mind at that moment, seemed like hundreds, if not thousands, of bees flying around the room. Despite the numbers being more than a slight exaggeration, she was so terrified of them that she could not return to the room to fetch her baby. She screamed for her friend, who had just arrived to see her and the newborn, only to find her friend just as afraid to enter the room. They both panicked that the bees would head over to the baby. In their frantic state, the friend declared she knew who could help. She figured that since I was, in her words, a *'bee whisperer,'* I was the only one who could help in such a situation.

It seems that when her husband left the house to fetch her from the hospital, he left the screen door open in his eagerness to go. Unbeknownst to him, there was a hornet's nest nearby. The number of hornets that had dropped in for a visit was, in fact, anywhere from seven to ten bees. I am sure the small creatures figured that since the welcome sign was up with the open door, why not? The homeowner felt that because of the baby in the room, she could not take a chance with her only weapon of choice, bug spray. I understood completely that it would be too harmful for a newborn's lungs, and since we had run out of options, I had no choice but to put my faith to the test and do my best in such circumstances. With no further hesitation, I gingerly stepped into the middle of the room and began to prepare for what I was sure would become a human and hornet battle. I could only hope they did not realize that my mind was racing with fear. I was just as scared as the other two humans in the other room and hoped that the hornets would not wholly pick up on my negative energy, certain that agitated vibration would rile them up in readiness for battle. Still, I felt someone had to do something, so here goes, ready or not!

Although it was a bit of a struggle to overcome those fears, I proceeded by speaking in a very soft voice, not so much for the sake of the bees but because I was not so eager for the women around the corner to hear what I was saying, especially if it did not work as planned. I turned my full attention to trying to picture a scene of a battle with the hornets, with me coming out as the winner and then immediately visualized a secondary option with them flying out the door to the freedom they came from. I explained to the tiny creatures that if they chose the battle scene, I would likely be wounded by their stings, although I was prepared for what would happen to me. However, they would need to keep in their teeny weeny, little minds that I was a giant to them, and no matter the difficulty, the outcome was a no-brainer. Ultimately, they would meet their demise, or…, they could leave peacefully, making everyone happy.

I went to great lengths to explain that this space differed from their regular territory outdoors where they belonged, and due to that fact alone, did they not realize the unfairness of terrorizing those who belonged inside the premises? I reminded them that the baby was an innocent bystander, not deserving of being separated from her mother, who was too afraid to come to the rescue. It was not fair for all concerned, and if they truly understood the goodness of a kind creator, they would appreciate that we came from the same source. I promised to give them a moment to pick which scenario best suited them before reaching for the swatter. My lecture was over, and I patiently awaited an answer, hoping they would give me a sign that they understood the options: death or freedom.

What happened next was as incredible of an outcome even to me as it was to the two women watching from the other room. The hornets gathered together in a small swarm and proceeded to fly closer, making me think at first that they chose to do battle. However, to my astonishment, they then organized themselves in a single-line formation and began to advance towards me only to fly around my head three consecutive times before flying straight out the door one by one. At that moment, my heart was filled to the brim with love and appreciation for what took place, not forgetting the sign of understanding that was presented. How could it not be anything other than a magical interconnection? My mind was reeling to such an extent of complete shock to what had just taken place.

I turned to see that the two friends, holding on to each other, were frozen on the spot, demonstrating complete bewilderment by what they had just witnessed. They stood with mouths agape, unable to speak. As I took my leave, admittedly in somewhat of a state myself and wanting to be alone to contemplate what had just occurred, I could only say to them both, *"Please don't tell anyone about what happened here; I don't want to be known as the crazy lady who talks to bees." "And besides, no one will believe you." "I can hardly believe it myself!"*

Story Reflection

Strange as it seems, once you experience such an unusual but seemingly natural connection as presented in this story, it is relatively easy to understand the 'marvellousness' in all things of nature, just as Aristotle indicated in the following quote. **"To understand is to know."** *From my personal experience in this story, his quote comes to life!*

The mind opens up to new understanding in situations such as what happened with the bees. If it had not happened, it would have been challenging to comprehend, let alone believe. No matter how often one hears about similar experiences, such communication with nature is difficult to understand, even during the experience itself, no matter one's belief in such matters.

To experience such a marvellous moment of communication with nature's beings, one must indeed be open to the possibility and willing to communicate in whatever manner is presented, just as Glenys Acorn relates in her prelude statement regarding these stories. At least, that is precisely the case in this buzzing bee experience.

ENCHANTING VISITOR

"Nature does not hurry, yet everything is accomplished."

-Lao Tzu

How often does one feel stuck or wholly caught up in situations seemingly out of one's control yet, for the most part, managed to snap out of the resulting doldrums reasonably quickly after something magical happens? This story speaks to just such a happening at a challenging time in my journey. It took place when a most peculiar feeling of being trapped in a dark cloud of doubt had taken control, overriding any sense of change with no escape to the negativity creeping into a once positive mindset. The magical encounter came as an opportunity that brought balance to my psyche, wonderfully appearing just as I was about to step out onto my balcony. It came in a purely 'unexpected' connecting moment while looking over the vista of this city's beauty, stopping by to rest for a moment or two in my garden retreat. I say magically because the appearance of relaxation and calm always arrived as if coming from a supernatural source.

This incredible story begins at a particular time when I was feeling overwhelmed with sadness while convalescing from a car accident that ended my career. Although I suffered only what was considered minor injuries that took some time to heal, my confidence took a beating that I could not shake off. I was left with a type of brain fog, unable to focus correctly. Hence, I had no choice but to end my established business by retiring early. I was thoroughly stuck in my misery, feeling helpless and disappointed. I could not tap into any of my previous appreciation for life's beauty in any shape or form. Like an unstoppable windstorm, my 'zest' for life quickly dissipated, leaving me convinced that the dark clouds of sadness were now part of my existence. In my despair, I remember calling out silently to the universe, how long can I stay in this misery? What can I do to make it stop?

Not much longer after my plea, an extraordinary moment of enchantment presented itself with a sudden flapping of wings that caught my immediate attention. My answer arrived on a very unexpected occasion, once more snapping me out of my doldrums. Now, I was accustomed to having little creatures, like small birds, spiders, bees, and bugs, drop by for a sporadic visit with me or, more accurately, my balcony plants. Up until this point in time, the most significant in size of a bird I have ever seen on my balcony railing has been a couple of crows. I can't say I am particularly fond of them, knowing that they are pesky birds that make annoying noises, lording it over the smaller ones as raiders of their nests in the spring months. I would often see shadows fly quickly onto the overhang of my balcony. Happily, those pesky crows use the roof of the building as their gathering stops, leaving my balcony as a resting stop for others.

I had long considered my balcony an inviting and pleasant space for most of the smaller species of birds visiting over the spring, summer and fall months. But what I was about to view at this extraordinary moment, looking out of the window from my living space, was utterly different. It seemed like a giant creature had fallen out of the sky and landed on my balcony railing. I could hardly believe what I was seeing before my very eyes. After getting over my initial amazement,

I gasped in awe and wonder at this majestic bird landing so close as if in preparation for a memorable visitor experience.

Once the shock of such a sight subsided, I tried to figure out what kind of bird had arrived, landing almost at my doorstep. In that magical moment, I could hardly comprehend how or why such a large bird dropped by, nor could I distinguish if this enchanting creature was a juvenile hawk or eagle, being so similar in stature during the early stages of growth. I did recognize it as a young bird because of the fluff at the top of its claws. I must admit I had never seen such a magnificent creature up close. Luckily, my camera was close by, and I immediately grabbed it and managed to snap a picture through the window of my balcony door. I would not let such an opportunity slip by as I knew without proof, no one would believe me. This was not a common occurrence by any stretch of the imagination, at least not in a city setting.

I did not go out on the balcony as I did not want to disturb the enchantment of such a visit nor scare it away, although due to its size, I am sure I would be frightened more than the bird. However, as I approached the window, it immediately turned its head and looked me straight on, eye to eye. I was sure that it knew I was there. At that moment, a lighthearted song passed through my mind; *I was looking back to see if you were looking back to see, it I was looking back to see if you were looking back at me."*

My appreciation for the mystery and beauty of nature had always brought solace and laughter to my heart in the past. This situation was no different, offering me a deep sense of lightheartedness, feeling a substantial fluttering leap in my heart at the moment of eye contact. I genuinely believe that it impacted a mutual recognition of enchantment to such a degree that something deep within me shattered into a thousand pieces, only to be replaced by a warm glow, as if a door suddenly swung open and filled the emptiness of purpose in my heart with light. Who would have believed such a thing could have happened in the blink of an eye?

While enjoying the regal presence of this large bird for a good bit of time, the exact minutes I could not say, although to me it seemed close to an hour before it flew away, I realized that my balcony was void of the usual charm that had always been part of the welcoming ambiance I had intended for anyone who stopped by for a visit. It was the middle of summer, and I still hadn't organized my retreat setting. Until that moment, I realized that I had not spent a moment in mindful appreciation of my outdoor space since the accident. I missed watching the seagulls and wild geese fly in circles in the open space just a stone's throw away. Sometimes, they flew so close you felt you could reach your hand out and touch them as they passed. I had not noticed the lovely sounds of spring melodies coming from the mating calls of the small birds, who often used the balcony railing as a calling point due to the strong acoustics at this location.

I should not have been so surprised that once more, nature would bring the answer that was staring me in the face all the time: my balcony. I don't know how I could have missed it since I only needed to open the door and step out. I had been so wrapped up in my misery that I did not take advantage of what was patiently awaiting my attention. What had happened to my plans for my yearly Zen Garden retreat? I knew what I needed to do. A trip to the garden centre was in order, so I headed out to purchase some beautiful flowers to add to what was missing.

I had to admit that the visit from this magnificent bird had been just the thing to shake me out of the emotional frump that had such a strong hold over me at the time. Once more I was amazed at how nature can come to the rescue even before you realize you need rescuing. This bird dropping by for a visit was a reminder to be open to the unusual frequency of energy that goes unseen the eye, but there nonetheless.

The next afternoon, just after I left my newly organized retreat, coming in to get out of the hot afternoon sun to get a large glass of water, I paused again at the window. To my astonishment, the enchanting creature had returned to the very same spot as the day before! Once again, as I approached the window, I was met with a turned head in acknowledgement of my presence. I was sure that during this time of connection, I glimpsed a twinkle of the eye in appreciation for my efforts. I do not know why my awareness turned to such a thought or even if gratitude was relevant from such a magnificent creature in this case. I did, however, sense that it welcomed my caution by staying indoors, giving it a moment or two of rest from those pesky crows sitting atop the overhang to my balcony.

I knew without a doubt that had I not been on the top floor of the building, this magnificent creature would not likely have chosen this spot as a sanctuary from the pesky crows following its every move. Now, I am sure the crows have their reasons, as this was a massive bird of prey to them. Honestly, what was taking place was all part of the natural order of things, but I still felt very privileged that such a large bird had chosen my balcony as a retreat. This time, the visit was indeed shorter than the day before. However, I did not miss a moment as I pulled up a chair to the balcony door and sat in pure enchantment for the next few minutes, enjoying the joy of merely watching. I was happy I managed to get another photo so my story would be believed when I told others about this visit. I must admit that I felt very privileged during this fantastic interlude with nature. At the time, I wondered…, how could it get any better than this?

I could hardly recognize myself after this second visit, knowing it was perhaps one of those once-in-a-lifetime happenings in one's journey. My mindset about life had made a complete turnaround, returning to a more positive outlook than I had been accustomed to for quite some time, and I knew that no matter what came next, I would be okay. It does not matter what future challenges I face; I will meet them with courage and strength, knowing it is all part of the journey. Everything for the rest of this second magical day went without mishaps, and my heart was filled with appreciation for all the beautiful things in my life. I would sleep well that night, knowing I would wake up refreshed and ready for a new day. At least I did not have pesky crows following my every move!

Early the following day, my husband called me to come to the dining room window and bring my camera. I could hardly believe what was awaiting my gaze. I was astonished by yet another visit from my enchanted visitor to my balcony. It was hard to think that this magnificent creature had returned. Once was terrific, twice was downright amazing, but three times…, miraculous! I instinctively knew that there was something different about the visit this time. It was at the opposite end of the balcony rails, and its stance was one of getting ready for flight, not a resting one. Thankfully, I obtained a couple of shots before it lifted up and away. I do not fully understand why I knew I would not see it again on my balcony, other than perhaps high in the skies above. However, deep down, I knew this had been an extraordinary, enchanting visiting experience.

There was no eye contact this time around. It would be the last time I saw this enchanting creature that answered my call for rescue. It seemed that as it took flight, it too had lifted off high into the sky with less burden. I did notice that no crows were divebombing or following. I like to believe that it flew with a lighter heart and that it, too, found strength and a bit of peace from the energy offered by my little Zen Garden.

Just as this magnificent bird soars high in the sky, with freedom beyond my comprehension, it still knows it must come down to earth occasionally for a rest. I will keep the lesson it presented to me close to my heart and mind. What stood out for me was that answers for all kinds of dilemmas or heartache are always closer than you think if you stop to pause, set your worries aside and go forward with the little things that bring love and peace to your mind. I learned the importance of grounding myself occasionally to help improve awareness and expand one's ability to overcome diversities and not be afraid to look for enchantment, knowing it will find you. But watch out for those pesky crows, which are sometimes most annoying.

Story Reflection

*From the first visit of this magnificent creature to the last, one cannot help but ponder how easily this story fits with the opening quote from Lao Tzu regarding '**timing**' and what is accomplished through nature.*

It sometimes seems that no matter the circumstances or what is needed in one's life, meaning flows, bringing solace to one's soul when least expected. Nature, indeed, does provide its gift at just the right time.

No matter the truth of how or why such a connection took place, each of nature's beings involved in the experience received a peaceful and enjoyable interlude that speaks to something bigger than self. Perhaps comprehending the occasion as more than coincidence is subject to one's belief that 'timing' was of the essence.

A SQUIRRELY BARGAIN

"Nature's lessons are timeless, teaching us patience, resilience,

and the beauty of embracing change."

-Gabriel Cruz

It all began on a late summer morning, a stark contrast to the busy life I had been leading. The realization dawned that there were fewer days left when the sun's warmth was thought to be so hot that one could not stay in it for too long. I had just realized I had been avoiding my meditative retreat area other than watering the plants. It had been a challenging year after the passing of a dear loved one, leaving me with a heavy heart and seemingly little time to stop and enjoy what was surrounding me. Keeping busy was the mode I was caught up in at the time. Blocking out much of my sadness was easier if I kept busy. After a quick peek out my balcony door, it became apparent that this would be one of those last sun-hot days.

It was the perfect time to take a short break from what I considered many crucial household tasks and enjoy some late morning sunshine before that dreaded noonday heat hit the balcony. There was only one place to go for such a well-deserved break. It was time to head out to what I like to call my balcony Zen Garden. After all, I had worked hard to make this space a sanctuary where I could meditate while enjoying the fantastic river park sights and sounds heard above the treetops. I am fortunate enough to have a bird's eye view of the city's eastern, southern, and western surrounding areas, and it allows me a splendid view of incredible sunrises and the breathtaking beauty of outstanding sunsets. What better way to appreciate all that surrounds me, no matter what has happened in one's life? It is a great location to be even while grieving.

My little balcony retreat also provides an exceptional resting area where I can occasionally appreciate the odd visit from nature's various flying and crawling tiny creatures that stop by to check out my plants. At certain times of the year, it turns out that I am not the only one who enjoys such sought-after peace during the early mornings before the city awakens. I am often blessed by a small colourful bird that drops by to rest on the balcony rails and sings me a heartfelt tune. Well…, I like to think the song is for me; however, since these visits usually arrive in early Spring, there is a strong possibility it may be a mating call. Nonetheless, it warms my heart and soul, and at this stage of life, I will take what I can, especially as finding the time to sit and appreciate this exceptional space has been little to none lately.

This day was perfect; after trying to catch up on some chores and finding the time to write, I would attempt to take a break during the kind of day that shade was the place to be for all creatures, great and small, including humans. Having allowed myself a limited time, with a cool beverage in hand, I headed towards the balcony before it became too hot, only to find a different situation begging my attention. Who would believe what my eyes were witnessing at the very top apartment of this building? To my utter surprise, as I approached the door, I found myself gazing at a small, and what could only be described as a bit scrawny-looking, black squirrel! This tiny creature was taking no notice of me as it was busily munching away at the interlocking foam mats that had been so delicately placed on my balcony. My mind could hardly grasp why this creature would be up this high, especially with it being the 11th floor and no trees in sight close to the building. Nor, for my life, could I figure out why it felt the need to be chewing away at the mats in the first place. I was left in a state of utter bewilderment.

Observing such a sight caught me entirely off guard, completely ruining the serenity of my retreat time, and my first instinct was to shoo it away. However, before doing so, I figured I needed to work out my frustration by giving it a piece of my mind. Determined that the situation was not something I could easily brush off, I stood at the balcony door and began my lecture in a calm but firm and unyielding voice that, I figured, spoke volumes: *"What in the world do you think you are doing?"* The squirrel looked up for a second or two, seemingly undisturbed by my voice or presence, and promptly returned to destroying my mats! A few untold descriptive words came tumbling out of my mouth that soon morphed into a lecture, if only to let this small creature know that the material was unsuitable for any nest building and…, if eating the material was the intention, a stomachache would surely result. There was no holding back from my monumental displeasure.

Feeling the need to get close and personal, at least close enough to present my argument for what I was witnessing, and just in case the creature did not hear me clearly, I stepped out onto the balcony to continue my tirade. What happened next could only be observed as a unique connection between the willpower of human and animal nature. Now, you would think that our difference in size alone should have created a sense of caution for such a little one, but for some peculiar reason, this tiny animal chose to stay to hear me out! Realizing that folks may think my intention to communicate with such a creature was acting foolishly crossed my mind; however, having had success with hornets (*a whole other story*), I figured, what the heck? If the squirrel was brave enough to stay, I might as well continue. This was my chance to establish a unique bond with a wild creature.

Since we are all connected to the life energies of this world, there seemed no reason not to take it a step further. Of course, I was thoroughly convinced that a meeting of minds could occur. Before proceeding any further, I sat on the balcony chair close to the door to pick up where I had left off. I immediately began presenting my concerns about the situation to the squirrel. To my amazement, in the blink of an eye, that squirrel hopped onto the sunbed just opposite me and stretched itself across the cushion, indicating that I had its full attention. There was no fear nor hesitation in this little creature's demeanour as it kept a steady gaze toward my ongoing speech. It was unlike any naturally cautious squirrel I had ever encountered. Like scolding a child, I calmly and firmly informed the squirrel that continuing this destructive behaviour would not do. There was no benefit in such distasteful conduct. It would only lead to a very angry human if it decided to continue.

I must admit that I was fascinated by this unfathomable reaction to the kind of attention it gave me. I could only surmise that the squirrel, with its unwavering gaze, was entirely engrossed, demonstrating a significant interest in what I had to say. An assumption had to be made that attentive listening was at its peak! My boggled mind soared with self-adulation, thinking my lecture was working, and I decided to present a most favourable trade-off for the destruction that had taken place with the mats. At the time, the damage was minimal, and if destroying my property stopped, I would provide it with a few nuts. How could it not resist such a bargain? Especially since everyone knows that the nuts would be more nutritious and, beyond a doubt, more suitable for the little one's digestive system.

As a matter of course, I explained the deal in greater detail several times before coming to a complete stop. During the offered bargain, that little creature stayed quietly stretched out as if listening to my every word. Timing was essential, and I had to be sure it fully understood such a generous offer. I even visualized the dear one sitting quietly, eating a variety of nuts that I knew I had stored in my cupboard. When finished, it was my turn to patiently wait for an indication of acceptance, and to my surprise, the squirrel jumped off the lounger and sat before me, looking up as if fully understanding my proposal. I could only surmise that it now patiently awaited evidence of my end of the bargain. I had no other option but to accept this reaction as an agreement and had no doubt by the little one's demeanour that the deal was indeed sealed!

I quietly got up and retreated indoors, only to return with a small bowl containing various seeds and nuts. The dear little thing was still sitting in the same place, tolerantly waiting for my return. As soon as I placed the bowl beside it, the darling little squirrel began consuming its prize without hesitation and, notably, I might add, very greedily. I smiled inwardly, pleased with myself, with all my good intentions and bargaining powers, believing authentic communication had occurred. An animal and human bargain had been successful, especially at my end. After all, a bargain was a bargain, and I was sure this little creature would follow through and leave once it had finished eating.

I watched in glee for a few moments before retreating into the apartment. To my way of thinking, leaving me with no doubts, I had witnessed and just experienced one of those rare energy exchange moments between human life and nature, linking together in real time. How could I believe otherwise? The entire event fits nicely with a strong connection possibility. And, of course, there was that hornet event long ago, but I digress. Heart-filled with pleasure at what had just taken place, I left my little friend busy consuming the spoils of the agreement and returned to my household chores.

After a time, I peeked to see if such a wise and agreeable creature was still there and to my amazement…, the little one was stretched out on the mat, just under the shaded part of the sunbed, taking a nap of all things! I must admit that I had never seen a squirrel napping, and for a split second, I wondered if I'd killed it! Could it have met its demise with the nuts coming so soon after eating parts of the foam mat? I had visions of a tiny stomach exploding with such a combination, and just as I was about to open the screen door to check, thankfully, I saw his ear twitch and the opening of an eye, letting me know not to worry. It was merely having a nap away from the hot sun that now covered a significant part of the balcony. I was relieved to find the squirrel deep in full relaxation mode, thinking all was well in my little corner of the world. I silently retreated, returning to my busyness with a head and heart filled with wonder and awe at the magic of this day.

After about half an hour, I decided to see if the sweet little creature was up for a meditative human connection. But…, to my utter astonishment, I stepped onto a balcony in disarray! I could hardly believe my eyes as my mind began reeling with discontent. The little rascal had made a complete mess by digging up and devouring a flower bulb from a small pot, and the beast… had the nerve to return to his previous task of further shredding my mat! I was not amused. I now say nothing more than a deal-breaker of immense proportion before my eyes. My thoughts turned to questions without answers. Could it be that it was not satisfied with my end of the bargain? Perhaps there was discontent with the number of nuts provided or the possibility of a few outdated ones in the bowl. I must admit that stale nuts were a strong possibility at the time. It could be said that too little thought went into this bargain of mine, but too late was the cry! I quickly stepped out and immediately returned to my earlier tirade, only this time… I am sure a much higher level of disappointment could be heard in my voice. I was not amused!

Surprised, sensing something was amiss, the little 'bushy-tailed rat' stopped his destructive activities and tried to scamper away, hiding underneath the sunbed after hearing and seeing my displeasure. An avoidance dance soon began as I moved the sunbed, and he quickly ran back and forth across the balcony a few times before scampering off down the brick of the building. On further inspection, I noticed that not only had the flower bulb been consumed (the only plant that could have been brought inside for the winter), but so had some lovely flower buds from a plant sitting on the little side table by the chair.

To add to my disillusion, I would need to clean up the bits of the chewed-up, thoroughly ruined part of the interlocking mat. And…, not to be forgotten, a great deal of dirt from having dug the bulb up from its pot plus…, an unfathomable amount of flower petals from my table plant strewn everywhere. What a mess it turned out to be! My previous moments of serenity and surreal mystical thinking were crushed. The charmed energy spell and the bargain I had made in good faith had been broken, and as a reminder that squirrels just cannot be trusted, I decided to take pictures of the mess. Unfortunately, having been so caught up in the beguiling quality of the event before this mess, I did not get a photo of the squirrel during its charming moments. A picture showing how attentive he was or even one of him napping would have been nice to add to this story if only to demonstrate the truthfulness of it all. But for now, it must remain a tale of a broken bargain with a cunning squirrel on my balcony, no matter the believability.

However, on the plus side, the cleanup saved me some time preparing the balcony for winter, so I should not complain quite so much. About a week later, I saw a squirrel tail flash by my door. This time, I did manage to get a quick photo before he disappeared, no doubt testing the human emotional waters. No harm was done during this short visit. However, after a thorough check on my return, I noticed a small, chewed portion of the remaining foam mat, leading me to a different conclusion that perhaps it was left as a reminder of future possibilities that could take place.

Life had settled, and I eventually moved past the absurdity of the incident and humility of a deal gone bad. After all, experiences with nature often have a peculiar way of teaching a lesson. Discovering the real lesson behind this one may take me a while. One lovely fall afternoon, something outside on my balcony caught my attention. It had been a few weeks since the unique visit from my squirrel friend. From the corner of my eye, I saw a black blur moving quickly past the window, and as I turned from my computer for a closer look, to my utter amazement, he was back! Only this time, he was busy digging in my plant pots for hidden treasures. I did not mind so much as the time to remove the slowly dying plants was approaching, knowing they would be replaced in late spring next year. I had since learned that a few lower apartment dwellers were feeding the birds and squirrels, leaving me to finally understand that many unannounced visits to my little garden had taken place long enough for peanuts to be buried in every pot!

He did not look quite as scrawny this time, although I gather his hunger got the best of him, so he returned knowing this human was an easy mark. He was fattening up for the winter and figured it was safe to retrieve his little hoard. Fortunately, this time around, my camera was at hand. I managed to get a photo catching in the act. He will probably not return for more visits with the peanuts gone and winter coming soon.

From my point of view, the moral of this experience is to be wary of agreements accepted by charming little creatures who have no qualms about breaking any bargains made by humans. But there's more to this story, more lessons to be learned. It will be interesting to see what happens next year in my little Zen Garden retreat and what new insights I will gain from these encounters.

Story Reflection

One can only hope that the craziness of this situation will not be repeated, at least not the destructive part of this particular 'interlude with nature.'

Although a mystery, it seems that Nature provides just the right experience to lighten one's heart during a difficult time. Each interlude brings a fuller understanding of this story's opening quote from Gabriel Cruz regarding the timelessness of what is offered through nature's means.

Experiencing the timelessness of nature's lessons is genuinely exacting. It teaches patience no matter the circumstances of encountering situations beyond control, at least at the beginning of a connection. No matter how it is delivered, considering what happened in this story, one can freely come to terms with embracing the need for change. So often in life, there is no choice but to embrace everything nature presents as a timely lesson.

FEATHERED CHARMER

*"Nature is the greatest classroom,
where every leaf, every bird,*

*and every ray of sunshine holds a
lesson waiting to be learned."*

-Gabriel Cruz.

This story involves nature interludes with what I like to think of as a very clever seagull. All story segments occurred during specific self-reflective periods through my journey, precisely four incidents of sharing extraordinary moments with a most charming, feathered friend who had come to my aid. Each event contained thought-provoking moments that could only fill one's heart and mind with awe and wonder. Although nothing in life prepares one for such interactions, experiencing them cannot help but expand one's appreciation for more unexpected moments. For me, self-reflection seemed to be the key that unlocked the enchantment of how I view life and nature that continues to the present day.

Part One

JOYFILLED INTENTIONS

It all began at the start of a unique summer, a time of self-reflection after the end of a complicated relationship. My mind was filled with thoughts of what had taken place and how things would go from a position of starting over while preparing to live on my own. After all that took place during such a dreadful breakup, I moved back to my hometown, a small city at the mouth of a river that flows into one of the Canadian Great Lakes. It was not necessarily an easy time for me, but I would have to come to terms with personal issues, nonetheless. Moving through the effects of my experience, I found myself searching out quiet spots of solitude to make sense of where I was going from that point on.

    Life was slowly changing after getting settled in a place of my own and a new job, so my sadness over the situation had begun to dissipate. It was time to look inward and reacquaint myself with my new surroundings to reestablish some lost feelings of joy. Something that had been missing for some time. During that first summer of my arrival, I often took an early morning walk in the park along the bay close to the donut shop, where I stopped for coffee and muffins on the way to work. I awoke this particular morning with a powerful urge to give back to nature something special, and for the first time, I bought a bag of day-old muffins with my coffee as an offering of thanks for what had given me so much pleasure over the past few weeks. I started my day earlier than usual and headed for my favourite observation spot by the bay. My mission… take the muffins to feed the ducks at the water's edge.

It was such a lovely summer morning, and I was determined to create a pleasant moment in my mind's eye with my generous offering while encouraging a joyful atmosphere for the ducks. I had found great enjoyment and relaxation for what I considered at the time, 'my shattered soul' while walking through the park's garden pathways and strolling around the bay watching the ducks, geese and seagulls of all sizes interacting and bobbing in the water. It was heartwarming watching the mother ducks and their ducklings flowing close behind swim along the water's edge. These early morning walks warmed my heart, giving me a sense that no matter what happens, life goes on.

On this particular morning, as I approached the railings by the waterfront, I saw several ducks paddling along the edge and figured it would be an excellent place to start. I had broken off a few pieces from the muffins and began to toss them down to the ducks; almost immediately, as I did so, a solitary seagull swooped down and caught the most significant piece before hitting the water. It had gobbled it up so fast and then landed close by on the railing, seemingly waiting patiently for me to give up my quest to feed the ducks and throw more its way.

I was miffed that it was so bold, so I turned instead to throw even more morsels at the ducks. At that point, another seagull quickly zeroed in on the chunk before the ducks could reach it. It seemed my mission to feed the ducks was making a quick detour, but I was determined that the greedy seagull would not win out, so I turned to walk further up the bay walkway to find another spot. As I began my mission, I could not help noticing that the first seagull was walking alongside me, still patiently waiting for another morsel to come his way.

Since the greedy one had disappeared, I decided to throw this charming one a chunk, and as I did so, it flew up to catch it in mid-air. Feeling inspired and smiling inwardly, I started playing a *'toss and catch'* game with the friendly seagull, forgetting all about the ducks. However, the next throw seemed to beckon to another of its kind. At that point, the play we had established became challenging for the first seagull as the newcomer was a more significant and faster bird at catching. This game remained fun until, a few moments later, when approximately fifteen seagulls flew in to see what was thrown. Although, at the moment, it seemed like one hundred! Before I knew it, they were getting closer and closer to me, holding the bag, and it soon became apparent that they fully understood it was the source of the food. There was no shooing away or stopping those birds from securing the bag's contents.

With this new turn of events, I quickly became panicky, and I had little time to figure out what to do as they were much too close for comfort. I did the only thing I could think of in such a frantic state: I threw the whole bag away from me onto the open grassy area. I immediately felt foolish, thinking, why did I not just empty the bag's contents into the water? At least then, my original intention of feeding it to the ducks would have been fulfilled. However, to my utter amazement, along with my initial thrust of the bag opposite the water, my ring flew off my finger. My first thought was, thank goodness I did not throw it toward the water that would have been my ring's watery grave. However, I felt even more foolish as my initial panic became a frantic search for my ring. I was thankful that the birds were preoccupied with battling each other in an eating frenzy, tearing apart the bag. I quickly turned towards where I thought my ring had landed but could not see it and, now in a panic, figured it was forever gone.

I began to wonder if there was enough time left to look. At that point, I was in quite a state, with such a close call from the seagull swarming attack and flying ring, both filling me with anxiety. What a dreadful ending to such good intentions of creating a joy-filled experience for me and the ducks! Now, not only did the ducks receive nothing, but I had lost a very precious possession that would be passed down to my daughter. My heart sank, and just as tears were about to come flooding through, I turned around to notice that the first charmer of a seagull was sitting quietly a few feet away from me. My first thought was, "*Look what you caused!*" until I realized that this fascinating bird did not join in the frenzy of the others, so I took a deep breath and smiled at the little fellow. I felt terrible that I had not thought to keep a portion aside for such a 'non-greedy' one and felt even more remorseful and, at the same time, astonished as I realized that he was sitting beside my ring. It must have somehow rolled that way, as it was in a completely different area from where I thought it had gone. I would not have even looked in that direction. As my ' champion ' took flight, I ran towards the location gratefully. As I picked up my ring, I sent a special thanks to the universe and extended what I considered a burst of gratitude from my heart to this most charming of birds.

Part Two

CHANCE MEETING ON THE HILL

It seemed that time had swiftly flown by, with my getting on with the challenges of settling in and before I knew it, summer was about to end, leaving few leisure days to find a quiet retreat to take in some sunshine and ponder the meaning of life, at least my perception of all that had taken place during the days that followed my first encounter with the seagulls. Soon, one would be caught up in the hustle and bustle of plans and preparation at home and work with the fast-approaching fall and winter seasons. There are people to see, places to go, and many things to do!

It was a warm and sunny Sunday when I next had some spare time on my hands. It was the perfect time to find a peaceful spot at my favourite park to enjoy some sought-after solitude, allowing me to be more receptive to whatever nature had in store. At first, on arrival, I thought my plan was foiled, seeing that many folks at the park seemed to have the same idea of taking advantage of such a fine day so late in the season. After a short time wandering through the park, my luck turned as I noticed that at the far end, no fellow humans were to be found at the top of the hill. I thought it was the perfect spot to sit silently while enjoying the abundance of nature, complete with birds, flowers, trees, and the beautiful blue sky filled with lovely fluffy white clouds. Perfection at its best to catch a few warm rays of sunshine during my mindful meditation moment on the hill. How could it get any better than that?

After a few minutes of settling in my spot, I became aware of a single seagull that had landed reasonably close to where I was sitting on the same hill. Perhaps it, too, was searching for a quiet place away from the busy crowds of humans and fellow birds. Although pleased that it had come to share in my meditative state of euphoria, a flash of my experience with the feeding frenzy meeting of the last bird of the same species momentarily passed through my mind. I immediately reminded myself that such an encounter would not occur as there was no food to share, and hopefully, this little one would not signal others to join him.

As I settled myself, letting go of any negative thoughts about birds, I figured that if I was not a bother to him, then there was no need to be bothered by its presence; hence, we both could share the space in peace. I sent a silent mind gesture of welcome to the seagull. My thoughts turned back to the moment's serenity, feeling calm and joyful at basking in the sights and sounds of nature. It was as if a beautiful bubble of pleasure surrounded me, and it soon became apparent that this charming little creature was feeling it as well. Whenever another bird was about to land on the hill, it would immediately exhibit territorial mode by flapping its wings while chasing it away, then gently landing safely and sounding a smidgen closer to me. If I did not know better, I would think I was being guarded and protected from outside interference that would take me away from my sought-after solitude.

This peaceful and calming moment lasted for about an hour, leaving me wondering if this charming little fellow was the same seagull that had helped me find my ring that strange day when I was trying to feed the ducks.? Now, that would indeed be incredible. I knew the chances of such a thing happening would be extraordinary and, of course, nigh toward impossible. However, in this case, and the most pleasant circumstances, I thought, why not? At that time, I felt as if a bond had occurred between us, so it was not too much of a stretch of my imagination to consider that this could be the same little charmer. At that time of my life journey, I recall feeling quite amused that at least interest in me and my well-being was being demonstrated in some form, and one must take admiration wherever and whenever it comes.

My solitude time was up, and as I arose to return to my busy world, it seemed that the seagull decided to return to its natural world simultaneously. Just before I chose to leave, I turned to the seagull and thanked it for sharing my amazing bubble of peaceful solitude and for being my guard. I waved goodbye, holding close a wish that we would, one day, meet again. At the same time, I shook my head and decided it might be time for me to connect with a human partner, as it seemed odd that I was so quickly being charmed by a bird. Since messages come in many forms, being nudged by nature seems entirely appropriate.

Part Three

SWEET AND LUCKY MOMENT

Fall had arrived with a flurry, leaving me little time to take myself to a place of solitude. I had returned to my human world feeling open and receptive to the possibility of someone special entering and sharing love, affection, and companionship throughout the second half of my life journey. I had finally come to terms with so many factors about myself over the last few years, learning that to be happy and whole, one must reach deep within the self and allow forgiveness for past mistakes. I also felt that happiness does indeed come from within. I was looking forward to all that my journey would bring. I had recently been approached flirtatiously and must admit that I felt inclined to flirt back. I needed to take the time to ponder on the arousal of feelings that began to surface. Perhaps my luck was changing, and my flirtation encounter was a sign of things to come, or was I merely living with a false sense of wishful thinking?

It was a beautiful day when the world around me was filled with the deep, rich colours of Fall, and I decided to take my lunch break at my favourite location, the park by the bay. I was pleasantly surprised at the sun's heat, so I settled for a quiet time sitting on a bench in the shade under the trees on the grounds. Besides, the walkway around the bay seemed busy, with many folks also enjoying the warm, sunshine-filled days before winter set in. I was looking for a more solitary space to contemplate my reactions to being noticed in a manner I had not been accustomed to for quite some time.

A dream-like quality took hold as I sat in solitude with my thoughts, and I figured my long-forgotten calming bubble of peace had returned. It was an incredible feeling, and I wanted to hold on to it as long as possible. It was one of those moments where my immediate surroundings took on a sense of sitting in the middle of a circle of blissful delight. A seagull landed a few feet away almost immediately after this enchanting moment began. I recalled thinking that my captivating charmer had returned within this heartfelt awareness. I could not be sure since all the seagulls seemed to look the same, and I, for one, could not tell them apart. However, at this point of interaction with a singular seagull in mind, how could it be anything other than my charming friend?

I did not hesitate to put the picture of our connection as friends in my mind and began speaking in a most endearing tone, welcoming it back. I chatted away with this charming companion about my appreciation for all our sharing moments. To me, they had been delightful experiences. It might come a little closer if it genuinely understood my thoughts. I was surprised as it came closer within a moment of projecting my thoughts in its direction. My heart warmed once more with gratitude that this special bird felt safe enough to be in such proximity and that if I wanted to, I could stretch out my foot and touch it with minimal effort. Not wanting to break the magical spell that had engulfed us both, I preferred not to put this gesture to the test.

With the bird so close, my eyes were drawn to the foliage around my feet. I slowly became aware that my feet were nestled in a patch of clovers, and my thoughts turned to the long-ago past as a child trying so hard to find a four-leaf clover and the disappointment of not being able to locate one. So many of my friends, even my brother, had found one, but not me. I could not help but think I was just not lucky enough to discover what I believed would make me happy. After all, everyone knew if you created a wish holding a four-leaf clover, there would be no stopping that wish from coming true. In childhood, such a mindset was considered *'magical thinking.'* As one grows up, one's perspective changes a bit, and it is safe to say that at this age and stage of life, I have reached a place long past childhood. Throughout my adult years, I felt trapped in the mindset of an unlucky person. This proved true in many ways, as I always had to settle for less. However, over the years of learning about life and arriving at the latter half of my adult journey, I intuitively knew that luck was not the culprit.

However, in this magical moment in time, as luck would have it, my charming, feathered friend moved a few bird steps closer to my foot,  and as my eyes followed its move, I found myself looking straight down at a four-leaf clover. My heart and mind did a joyful flip with astonishment and excitement at such a find. Somewhere deep within, at that inner child level, I gleefully accepted a new truth that my luck had indeed changed, and with such a change of heart, things would fall into place as they should. I marvelled at the mere coincidence of my feathered charmer friend once more directing me to what was within my grasp all the time.

One can only marvel at such a gesture that could so easily have been missed during this natural connection with nature, especially when simple messages are indeed recognizable from so many sources. Communing with nature can bring solace to the soul if we pause long enough to take it all in. And, of course, one cannot dismiss the wisdom of such a charming, feathered companion as my friend the seagull. I had much to be thankful for in the long run, even considering many of my mistakes in life. So much was learned through them. Here I sat with my newly acquired treasure, an unbelievable childhood prize of a long-wished-for four-leaf clover, and from that moment on, I truly believed in what I have often tried to convince myself many times over… that *"All is well in my world."* It certainly was at that moment.

From that day, I knew without a doubt that no matter what came in my life or where my journey would take me, it would be for my better good. It was time for me to relax and be at peace with the understanding that something good awaited me just around the corner. I sat in the loving embrace of the moment for about twenty minutes as if I was in a magic spell of appreciation for all that was, all that is and all that is to be. Then, in the blink of an eye, my little companion flew off, breaking the spell, and I bid my little charmer good travels until we meet again.

Part Four

DISTINCTIVE FAREWELL

Many years have passed since the last memorable interlude with my feathered charmer. Time has brought many changes, filling my life with the kind of pleasure and joy that I thought had passed me by. One of the most remarkable things was finding and accepting an extraordinary partner who filled all my hopes, dreams, and desires for a loving relationship beyond anything I thought possible. Life for me had changed for the better, and although much busier than anticipated, I had to admit I missed my solitary visits to the park. At least my loving man and I were fortunate enough to eventually settle in an apartment across from my favourite park with a balcony view of the river and bay.

In the late spring and early summer, I would spend time and make a meditative retreat on my balcony, which I liked to call my Zen Garden. It was a place where I could sit and enjoy a moment or two in mindful appreciation for what I had achieved through some challenging moments that come and go in any life journey. All my efforts to improve my life worked well for me, including many joyous times spent with my family, having my girls live in the same city, challenging work, and ever-adventurous travels with my loving partner. Life was good, and I did not doubt that it would continue in all the ways that brought me happiness for many years. That little four-leaf clover was still working its charm.

During one of my meditative moments, I watched a seagull soaring high in the sky, and my thoughts returned once more to my charming, feathered friend. It seemed that the soaring seagull had also found joy beyond understanding. As I watched, I was reminded of the book called **Jonathan Livingston Seagull** by **Richard Bach**. It is a whimsical tale that speaks to one's heart and mind, indicating that there is more to this living than meets the eye. This truth is demonstrated by a special Seagull that is no ordinary bird. He holds firmly to the belief that it is every gull's right to fly high in the sky, reaching for the ultimate freedom of challenge and discovery, finding his greatest reward in teaching younger gulls the joy of flight and the power of dreams.

Like Jonathan, my little feathered charmer had grown and found joy in flying higher than ever. In the book, Jonathan flies so high that he disappears, and lo and behold, as I watched my seagull fly higher and higher, in what seemed a fairylike instant…, he vanished out of sight. I could hardly believe my eyes and was puzzled by what I had witnessed as the sky was clear with no mist or clouds to obscure one's sight. How could this be? Were my eyes playing tricks on me? I remained focused on the area to see if my seagull friend would return, but I did not notice if he did. My only take on this enchanted moment is that there truly is *"more to this living than meets the eye."*

Despite seeing so many seagulls flying close to my balcony and beyond over the years, being so close to the bay, I have not felt a connection like the one I had with this intriguing bird. To my mind, my feathered friend said goodbye that day, knowing that we had indeed found what we were searching for… the joy of being alive, experiencing and living life to the fullest.

When writing my story, I looked up the longevity of seagulls and found the following information with a Google search. I admit I was as surprised as many of you might be at some of the information I found regarding these exceptional birds. I must admit that nature continues to surprise and amaze and remains a wonder to behold as we open our hearts and minds to all it brings.

- **How long do seagulls live?**

According to some experts, seagulls have a natural lifespan of about 20 years, and many records of seagulls have reached 25 years or even more.

- **Seagulls and cleverness.**

It is not well known that seagulls are very clever birds. They can learn new things throughout their lives and remember things for a long time. Some can even pass on their knowledge and behaviours to other seagulls.

There was much more information from my search, but I will leave it up to those interested in researching independently. Seagulls are a fascinating species to study.

INTERLUDES WITH NATURE

And so, my dear readers, with so many possibilities available to us in a lifetime, this intimate connection with nature could undoubtedly have been with one particular seagull. You have to admit he does seem to stand apart and certainly takes on the persona of a charmer. You can almost see that clever twinkle in his eye. What do you think? Something to think about, eh!

Story Reflection

Undoubtedly, the enchantment experienced from the segments of the feathered charmer, as presented throughout the various connections, played an intriguing role in the learning process over a significant period.

The lessons learned through the unique individual connections made in the story relay to us all the significance of what can be learned in nature's classroom, as stated in Gabriel Cruz's quote. "Nature is the greatest classroom, where every leaf, every bird, and every ray of sunshine holds a lesson waiting to be learned.."

No matter what is happening in one's life, if we are open and receptive to what nature has to offer, lessons filled with meaning are easily accessible from our surroundings, no matter where we find ourselves.

Perhaps the solace we receive through nature is always available and meant to be part of our experience throughout our life journey after all...

A SWEET SHARING MOMENT

"In the open air, our senses awaken, and we become attuned to the

intricate wonders that surround us."

-Gabriel Cruz.

Ellen's Story

I was asked if I had ever experienced an unexpected interlude with nature, and if so, would I mind sharing the circumstances, where and when? The experience that comes easily to my mind triggers a pleasant memory from a few years back of an interlude with nature during a particularly euphoric period of life, feeling the kind of complete peace and tranquillity that isn't easy to describe; however, since it seemed somehow connected to the enchantment of my nature encounter, it is hoped that the following story will try to do it justice. This narrative merely attempts to portray a segment of that experience.

Our city has several lovely parks offering citizens many opportunities to commune with nature. One of my favourite parks is located near a bay, which provides a peaceful escape from the chaos and busyness of life every season. In the late spring, summer, and early fall months, I would do my best to make the most of this tranquil space, providing me great pleasure when I could take advantage of what was so readily available. Our city is located beside a bay inlet connected to the river that flows from one lake into another as part of the Great Lakes system. The park area encompasses this busy waterway offering various sites, such as water sports and numerous big ships passing along the river. It enables easy access to watch the comings and goings of leisure boats while using the bayside docking area. It is also a great place to sit and enjoy all the sights and sounds from waterway action during the summer and fall.

The park also provides a great place to catch a glimpse of wild Canadian geese using the calm inlet waters, seagulls, and different types of ducks, taking advantage of the safety offered in and around the bay. In the late spring, the waterfowl are often accompanied by young ducklings frolicking in the water or following behind their moms over the park grounds. In the fall, it becomes a gathering place for the geese in preparation for winter flights to warmer destinations. Often, folks would come by to feed the ducks or watch them leisurely floating by while standing by the rails or using the benches along the walkway. The whole area is a most enjoyable setting for merely spending time people-watching or leisurely sitting and watching the splendours of nature that bring so much pleasure to one's soul.

The walkway around the bay is a popular spot for folks walking their dogs, lovers walking hand in hand, enjoying the sights and sounds of the bayside, and people riding bikes or whipping by on roller skates. You could easily hear the magical sound of children playing in the playground across from the walkway at the far end of the bay. Often, you would see folks strolling on the smaller walkway that wound around the flower beds throughout the park. It is the kind of park that, no matter the age and stage of life, has something to provide that can brighten the day and warm the heart to what Nature offers.

Also found on the park grounds is an open area where folks can enjoy the grounds for picnics between the trees or in the open field area, attending various events that include yearly fundraiser fairs, music concerts, and car shows. Around Christmas, while strolling through a trail of lights, lost in a world of unique music and seasonal displays, the atmosphere fills your senses with magic, regardless of age.

There was a time a few years back when one could enjoy a solitary moment or two sipping various types of teas at a little café, allowing a spectacular view of the park's amenities by the water. Occasionally, I would quietly sit in solitude, sipping raspberry tea and enjoying a piece of strawberry cheesecake topped with whipped cream. This delicacy was readily available at the café for folks who would come and make the most of the sunshine on the patio or sit inside to cool off. It also offered a place for anyone at the park to use the facilities while gathering at the picnic tables at a shady spot on the grounds.

The inside of the building was just as enchanting since it was built in a circular style with huge, picturesque windows along the bay side of the building, allowing the outdoor scenery to be part of its décor. During the summer months, many children were seen enjoying an ice cream treat sitting inside the café by the windows or outside on the patio. Seeing all this park had to offer from the little café that, unfortunately, has long since been torn down was one of those pleasures that will not be easily forgotten.

I often found myself sharing the café space with others, taking in the day's beauty, and enjoying lunch or other delicious treats from the menu. One of the hazards of eating on the patio is the occasional visit by the local bee population that seems to fully understand when the treats come out, whether welcomed or not by the humans. It could even be seen as a most comical show of perseverance to see who will outlast whom as they would zoom in for the delicious spoils of combat. Anyone who has eaten outdoors could attest to such a calamity, especially in the case of pesky wasps who take no notice of human displeasure. These little creatures are not frightened off by waving hands and arms, attempting to swat them away, nor disturbed by the odd sandal used as a weapon of war. I have even witnessed a patio clearing due to so many bees wanting to share in the delicious food, driving folks indoors to finish without the warfare chaos that takes place with their unwelcome visits with the bees.

My interlude with nature, which I refer to as the central part of my nature story, happened when I was enjoying one of those lovely days filled with what could only be described as *'the peace that passes all understanding.'* It was a perfect summer day to stop by the café and enjoy my favourite treat while absorbing the park's atmosphere. Walking towards the café, the surroundings seemed to take on a unique, almost unworldly radiance from the trees, plants and even from the grass where children played between the park's shade trees close to the building. In my mind, it seemed to set the stage for peace and serenity for humans and all of nature. It certainly fits nicely with the tranquillity I was feeling at that time.

I gathered my purchase of soothing fruit tea and delicious cheesecake and went to find my usual spot on the patio. The patio was not too crowded, and I had doubts that I would have been bothered even if it were, nor would I react to any invasion by the bees. The way I felt then, nothing mattered as the vibrational energy I was experiencing would not allow any interruptions to my peace of mind. My consciousness was in total harmony with the world. Besides, is it not true that all nature is sensitive to the energy vibration one gives off? From what I have witnessed about human nature thus far, it is well-accepted that 'energy' plays a significant part in fear response to encounters with nature. However, at that point, all I knew was that I felt too calm and was oblivious to any negative vibration entering my vicinity.

Within a few moments of sitting down and turning to my food and drink, I realized a single bee had flown into my space and landed on my plate. As it landed, I felt only a surge of goodwill, knowing it would not interfere with the depth of peace and harmony I felt then. As I took a sip of my tea and a bite of my cheesecake, I noticed that the bee began to show interest in what was being served. Strange as it may seem, at that instant, with my heart opened and filled with love for all of life, it was only natural and most appropriate to share some of what brought me so much pleasure. I sectioned off a piece of cake on my plate with a drop of tea and gave it peace during this exceptional sharing experience. The little creature did not bother me, and I felt no inclination to shoo it away. We sat silently together, enjoying our cake without any bother, as if we were the only ones in the sitting area.

I had long surmised the little creature decided to join me and share in the solidarity of the moment. I cannot say I was overly surprised that it joined me, nor would I be taken aback if it had been I who joined the bee. It seemed more of a mutual arrangement, as if we were both caught in the bubble of shared existence, enjoying a few blissful moments in the peace and harmony of our surroundings. No matter the reason, we knew everything was right in both worlds. All I can say about what was happening at that moment was that we were in tune and accepting of each other. It was the most natural thing to enjoy each other's company. We remained in this blissful bubble for about an hour before the little bee flew off into its world of nature, and feeling completely satisfied and refreshed, I slowly rose from my spot, ready to return to mine. I knew without a doubt that this unique moment would stay forever in my mind as a reminder of the intertwined connection to available harmony. Although I have yet to experience such a state of heart and mind as I was experiencing at that time of my life, I am encouraged that there will be a time when all humanity can experience such a state and live in a harmonious world of existence. If the bee and I can share, then how can it be otherwise? There is always hope.

CHALLENGING INTERLUDES

"In the wilderness, we learn the power of adaptation, as every step brings new challenges and opportunities for growth."

– *Gabriel Cruz.*

THE PERCEPTION OF GIANTS

"Nature is loved by what is best in us."

- Ralph Waldo Emerson.

The perception of 'giants' within the segments of this story refers to those perceived to be higher in status or more significant in body, mind and influence. Sometimes, being a giant is like holding power over someone or something, not always intentional but to gratify a deep-seated need for satisfaction, no matter the cost to another's well-being. In this circumstance, it would be considered acting more like a bully. However, the one who must provide homage may see the so-called bully as more unapproachable or unbeatable while having the power to lord it over them, much like a giant would undoubtedly be if they lived or shared space with humanity and the world of nature. For the victims, treading softly becomes the only means of escaping displeasure.

Part One

A CHILD'S VIEW

Growing up in an army camp away from any town or city influence and surrounded by farmland and ample wood acreage provided an ideal space for young minds to grow and expand. Growing up in such surroundings, one had ample opportunities to explore nature's wonders and, simultaneously, become consciously aware of 'gianthood,' at least regarding some aspects of human nature. This observation is especially valid, having lived among those who perceive themselves as 'overlords' due to rank and position in a confined encampment. This conclusion is based solely on a child's perspective while living and playing in such an environment without fully understanding all that encompasses growing up within the confines of an army camp. I had no idea at the time of all that was provided within the boundaries of this camp, made up of an essential service force supporting our country before and right after World War II.

Many bold and subtle hints regarding superiority presented themselves over those early army camp childhood years. Coming from one of many lower-ranking service families, the hierarchy cues were impossible for any child to miss. I could not recall any questions about higher-ranking officers and their families receiving a higher quality and quantity of goods and services; it was a given. The most significant difference between the *'haves and have-nots'* in my world was demonstrated through food and living space and reinforced in a child's mind by a few of the officers' kids, who took full advantage of any opportunity to remind you of their ranking superiority. Evidence of such differences in 'stature' came quickly once you were old enough to be away from the close eyes of parents and free to explore life on your own. Whether in the schoolyard or out exploring your surroundings, you quickly learned which side of the fence you belonged based on how a few kids perceived their 'superior' status.

I am not sure how the adults felt about such things during those growing-up years, but from a child's worldview, we were very much aware of who the boss was during those days in play. There were benefits, however, to belonging to what the kids perceived as 'lower-class' camp citizens. For one, we were in the majority, and our minds were not bogged down by constantly having to prove our worth based on our father's rank. Instead, we were at liberty to play and explore our space with a freedom not always given to those who were constantly trying to live up to a standard set by their parents, expecting them to set an example. It looked suspiciously like the higher-ranking fathers may have brought a higher anticipation of perfection into their households. From a kid's perspective, the higher the rank, the more nervous the child, searching for ways to work out their frustration on others. And what better way than to take it out on those they perceived as deserving of being put in their place? After all, it was an army camp, and their fathers always gave orders to other kids' parents, so it seemed reasonable for them to try it over their fellow playmates.

The downside of being on the lower end of the scale was that if we looked like we were enjoying ourselves too much, it was often construed as grounds for taunting or some torment that usually followed from the frustrated ones. One could easily consider a mindset of seeing them as giants overseeing inferior people who must do their bidding. Frankly, those who thought themselves superior were disregarded and ignored by most of us, leaving the others to join us in our play. Through play, things evened out nicely despite an odd reminder by some that they deserved more respect in some fashion or another. Even as a child, I was not sure this sense of superiority was intentional, but it occasionally showed its ugly head as part of its personality. Even the 'giants' in our growing-up world were not always aware of such character flaws due to coming naturally from such a socially structured environment.

No matter any character flaws, I was fortunate that my best friend was an officer's kid. She was an only child, whereas I was one of four siblings. I was used to having less but felt sorry for her as I had more with all that comes with having siblings, which, in my young mind, more than compensated for having to share our meagre resources. On the other hand, my friend was spoiled with little concept of 'sharing' as she pretty well was given everything she desired. She even had a very peculiar pet, a skunk, unheard of in my circle of friends. The rest of us did not even have a dog as a pet, perhaps due to extra costs or possibly another one of those ranking rules, as the only ones with them were from the higher-ranking families. Cats, of course, were a different matter altogether as most of the kids in the camp claimed a cat as their pet, although camp cats seemed to live independently, living mostly outside except in the winter months. They were smart to attach themselves to families, assuring a safe place to live when the weather turned nasty.

My special friend seemed to enjoy my company as she wanted to be 'in charge' and have someone she could boss around a bit. She liked her higher 'status' and never fully understood my willingness to be her friend. First, I felt sorry for her for not having an older brother and younger sisters to play with when she felt lonely. As my friend, she automatically qualified to come under the umbrella of the protection provided to me by my brother. In return, I was more than happy to receive some of the abundance readily available to her. It was a given that she would receive a soda and ice cream from the 'Officers Messhall,' which was available through a special pass from her father. I fully understood and accepted that the officers' families had more, such as oranges, bananas, butter, and many snack foods that we only partook of on special occasions such as Easter, Thanksgiving and Christmas. At the time, I was unsure why or how it was that way, but being her friend had enough benefits that made her 'bossiness' tolerable.

My best friend indeed was, in my young mind, a 'friendly giant' most of the time who went out of her way to keep me close at hand as most of the other higher-ranking officer's children were boys and, without any qualms, could be as mean to her as the rest of us. Her father was not the highest rank in the camp, and since the hierarchy of superiority was also displayed among the officers' kids, she was also a target of the few. It would take a while over the years of growing up, with play and exploration in the confines of the camp, for me to learn that all is not what it seems. Life and learning can come from the most unusual of circumstances. This friendship was ideal for understanding that not all superiority was equal, which was fully demonstrated by an incident at my friend's home.

It began during a moment in preparation for a most delicious treat. Before accepting any treat, my friend needed to put it to her deserving test by measuring portions of whatever was being served before I could take possession. In the mess hall, she would put the soda bottles together to measure in case mine was a minuscule more than hers. Of course, the most significant portion would need to be hers, and as soon as her parent left the room, the quantity of whatever we were given was up for her inspection. I did not mind this display of her making sure I did not receive more, as I was just happy to partake in something out of my reach in the first place. Besides, keeping the status quo and living peacefully was well-accepted. After all, was it not a fact in nature that 'giants' required more? Why would it not be accurate in my little world if it were not confirmed by nature? I took it for granted that this was how it was supposed to be and that her parents were not opposed to her superior behaviour. I was about to find out that this thinking was not altogether correct on my part.

In this particular incident, her mother had made us each a banana split. When her mother left the room, my friend reached across the table for mine and proceeded with her measuring procedure. However, her mother returned to the room during her inspection. After observing her daughter's deserving decision, she did not say anything but casually grabbed the can of whipped cream and walked over to my designated plate. Her mom slowly piled my portion with an unsurmountable amount of whipped cream, then gently slid it back in front of me. I thought my friend was about to explode with fury, as demonstrated by a face as red as a ripe cherry. I waited a fraction of a moment before digging into such a marvel of a treat, wondering if I should give it to my friend as soon as her mom left. That thought disappeared as fast as it arrived. Her mother stood close with arms crossed, waiting for me to start eating. I wasted no more time as I quickly dug into the sundae with an urgency never before experienced in my young life. Of course, I did not look in the direction of my friend as I knew she was not pleased. I could feel the vibration of her anger piercing my very being and instinctively knew that things would not go well for me if I stayed much longer. So, as soon as I finished, down to the last speck, licking my lips, I excused myself, saying I had to leave early. I was confident about what this playtime would be like and was not interested in testing my instincts. I knew that the 'giant' in my friend was crushed, and someone would need to pay the price.

Part Two

TWO FACETS OF BECOMING A GIANT

I had to admit that while heading home, I felt very smug, as demonstrated by the broadest grin ever pasted across my face, much like the Cheshire cat in the story of Alice in Wonderland. Complete satisfaction was bringing home this cat, leaving me to wonder if our pet cat felt the same after catching mice! Since it was still early, I took my time walking, and while basking in self-satisfaction, something taking place on the ground caught my attention. At first, I could not believe my eyes. I was looking at a parade of small pieces of bread moving toward a larger-than-usual colony of anthills. With curiosity getting the best of me, I sat down on the boardwalk to get a better look. I was utterly amazed at one of nature's extraordinary happenings in the bug world. In my mind, this was even better than the treat I had just devoured, finding great pleasure in watching or examining the goings on of birds, bees, flowers, or even trees, all part of the fascination of living on this planet in a world of nature.

As I recall, I became fully enraptured with the hundreds of ants marching in a straight line, each carrying a small piece of bread. My mind exploded with questions about such a task. Why and where were they headed? I guessed at the time that they had a fondness for bread.

Based on my knowledge about colonies of ants at the time, they were merely taking it to feed the younger ones hidden deep in the lower parts of the ant hill. Now, at this point, I must admit I wondered if they were aware of me watching them. I pondered for a bit if it were possible since they were so tiny if they see humans as a whole person in the form of a giant fumbling around in their world or, perhaps we humans would be seen only as a dark, heavy blob that suddenly appears, blocking the sunlight. Were they even aware of the destruction that we humans can reap upon them without a thought for their safety, leaving them no time to prepare? My mind swirled with how much they resembled humans as it was like watching a little army marching but carrying bread instead of rifles, much like the parades held at the camp. I wondered if they had a ranking system in place and if they had to endure bullies as giants amongst themselves.

After ten or more minutes, lost in my imagination, I wondered if anything would deter their determination to complete their mission. I placed a twig across their path to see what they would do. My meagre attempt to interfere seemed insufficient to change the line in the parade as they merely climbed over the twig. Not completely satisfied with my experiment, my next move was to replace the twig with a small rock. I do not know why I would be surprised with the same result of them simply crawling over it. With my curiosity running amok, I combined a few twigs scrunched together to make a wall. I was trying to figure out if they would take an easier route and choose to go around it versus the harder one climbing over, carrying what must have been considered a heavy burden as those pieces of bread were considerably more significant than their tiny bodies. To my utter amazement, they chose to climb up and over, staying true to the marching lane in place. There seemed no other route than what they had established, leading straight towards the ant hill quite a few inches away. These little critters were stubborn.

While trying to deter them from their mission, I wondered if they saw me as a cruel giant causing havoc in their world. It was not my intention to be so; however, I knew I was interfering with their life to such a degree that it was harder to accomplish their goal of reaching safety in the home colony as quickly as possible. I was deep into my 'giantism' dilemma before I noticed a more significant problem entering and disturbing my investigational interlude with nature. It soon became apparent that what was about to happen became even more detrimental to these ever so tiny creatures as who should appear, a couple of the giant 'bullies' from my world, who decided to come and see for themselves what was contributing to my tranquillity.

Now, these boys were known to gain much amusement, making girls run home crying, and they were about to find success once more in their mission, for as soon as they realized I was enjoying watching the ant colony at work, they promptly started to trample every ant hill in sight. I was devastated knowing that had it not been for my interest in the little ant kingdom below my feet, those boys would not have even noticed, and the tiny creatures could have gone on their mission without any undue cruelty of a couple of mean human giants. My curiosity brought not only roadblocks but destruction into their lives. I left in tears.

The next day, I promptly returned to see how the ants made out. I was hoping that they would have all survived. Although I did not expect to see a moving bread trail again, there were no signs of bread. However, I did see many more ants, too many to count, busily rebuilding their homes. I was happy that they did survive and was taken aback by the resiliency of such tiny creatures. One could only show admiration for a world so often destroyed by unexpected human events, let alone having to survive in a world where they are not seen or considered in the everyday lives of humans. Did they even know if we existed or if the havoc we created was to them like the unexpected natural events of nature that humans frequently must endure, like germs, floods, high winds and storms bringing destruction or merely playing havoc in the world we live, sometimes without a moments notice?

Part Three

GIANT IN MIND OR DEED

The next few years went quickly, paying little attention to imaginary thoughts of giants or my adventure with ants, until I found myself once again mesmerized by something that triggered my curiosity and brought it all back to memory. It was brought on by watching a TV program about an unusual possibility of how massive and miniature sizes could or could not co-inhabit. Once more, I wondered if humans are merely a tiny portion of something too large to grasp. Perhaps we are so teeny-tiny that we are living on the arm, leg or even finger of someone or something so massive, who perhaps is the very God we know and speak about but cannot see because he is beyond our comprehension.

The program in question was called 'The Twilight Zone.' Based on my memory of the story, it goes something like this. The scene opens with a rocket ship crashing on an unknown planet, and two astronauts who survived the crash landing find themselves in a world they soon discovered was barren of similar human culture. It seemed that they managed to get off an SOS before crashing and received a message back that there would only be one chance of rescue due to the distance, leaving them in survival mode and needing to make the best of their situation for many months before they could be reached.

The two humans made the best of the situation with supplies they saved from the wreckage. It soon became apparent that with hard work, they could survive as water and edible foliage were readily available from their surrounding world of nature. Not too long after crashing, they came across a colony of tiny human-like beings during one of their excursions into the forest. At first, they merely observed how the population lived. The astronauts were very large in comparison, so much so that the little people did not notice them watching. Because of all the similarities, they were fascinated with their find, knowing they must not interfere or make themselves known not to disrupt the newfound little domain's evolution. Although tiny, they were, in fact, very similar and lived in a primitive society, very much like the early days of humans with farms and a couple of small town-like villages. It seemed they routinely had rituals and worship services acknowledging an unseen deity.

Their observation continued until one of the humans felt the urge to interfere to see how they would react to whatever obstacle he could find to deter them from their everyday lives. He soon went far beyond observation mode and found amusement in the havoc he could cause without them knowing where it was coming from. There was so much pleasure to be had that he started spending more and more time close to the tiny colony. He was beginning to feel more like an invisible god, leaving him to wonder how they would respond if they knew he was the cause of the type of destruction he was reaping upon them occasionally. It did not take long before the man who considered himself now as a 'giant' among men was spending all of his time looking over the colony; however, the other human astronaut was not of the same mindset and stayed closer to the ship, not wanting to miss the relief party. He would check up on his companion from time to time to make sure he was okay. He was concerned but could no longer stand by watching what was happening with his fellow companion.

Since the tiny colony was quite a hike into the forest's interior from the ship, the astronaut was no longer interested in observing his companion. After several attempts at pleading with him to leave his 'giant god-like' human status, he decided it was best to leave him alone. This human giant was becoming more lost in his ego trip of being god-like, and because of becoming so lazy, he could not look after himself. He soon found it beneficial to let one of the tiny people know of his existence. Of course, with this knowledge coming from one little person, a hierarchy was soon set up within the colony, and the astronaut was seen as a vengeful god whose bidding had to be a priority. This human giant was so enthralled by how things were going that his ego expanded to the extent of needing worship. These tiny folks must now do what they can to appease him to be safe. He was now considered their god, and all his needs were addressed. The giant was very content with the 'status quo' he had established.

All was indeed well in the giant human's new world, and this system of things went on for many months with little to no effort on his part to look after himself. There came a day when the other human came rushing up to him to tell him that the rescue ship was about to land and that he would need to come quickly if he wanted to go home. He was warned that there would never be another ship to come to that part of the universe, so there would be no other means of escaping this world if he did not come now. This 'giant' human, accustomed to idolization, knew this would not be his status in his home world. He was determined to stay where he would be obeyed and worshiped. The temptation was too great. He stayed behind to enjoy his godlike status.

Happy and contented was he for many a month, until another spacecraft crash occurred in the same vicinity as the last one not far from this human want-to-be giant god. However, this time around, would you believe it, two astronauts stepped onto the scene, identical in every way and circumstance, except they were so massive they were 'giants' compared to the only human-like creature they found on the planet. This time, however, they were so big that they could not even see the tiny people since they would be like ants and of no interest to them, but they had no problem seeing the little human who now was in no way considered a god by them. The strangest part of the new scene was the indication that one of the 'giants' held the same mindset as the now little guy who would need to do his bidding to stay alive for as long as they were sharing the same space.

It remained a mystery if he would be enough to make the new 'god' like giant stay if rescued or if he would take the little guy back to be a servant for his remaining lifetime. All was left to one's imagination as to how it would turn out in the end, but for sure, one is left with much to think about in the world of giants and the kind of treatment provided to all lesser in stature. It certainly gives one much to ponder living in this world of nature and humanity, curious to explore beyond what we now comprehend and see.

GOING WITH THE FLOW

"A miracle constantly repeated becomes a process of nature."

-Lyman Abbott

FEELING THE ENERGY FLOW

BY LENA PARKER

I sit by the stream in awe of the movements that seem to flow in one direction and do not turn back the way it has come. It does not wait for the water behind. It does not question what is ahead.

Is there something it seeks, or may it turn around when I am no longer in its occupancy?

How can something in all its simplicity be so mending?

Perhaps there are the souls of those before me who drift here – flowing with the stream in the same direction, corresponding into one. Do they not concern themselves with where they have come from? Are they looking for where they have been?

Or do they find themselves indifferent to life's previous encounters, choosing to feel the flow of tranquillity with the stream—or is this simply destined to be?

I put my fingers in the water. It is accepting and remains consistent, even after I have chosen to place myself in its space. It flows around me, choosing not to delay. It is strong.

I ponder how something that flows with such a power feels so effortless – so serene.

I grasp the fact that a moment could make one feel whole. For an instant, I seemed to disregard all the agony my soul had felt in this lifetime. Will my soul one day join the streams?

Must you be guileless to inhabit your next life here?

Nonetheless, at this moment…, I am safe.

SWIMMING POOL WONDERS

I grew up feeling a strong relationship with water. Being born in a small border city close to a river that flows into a lake set the stage for my water connection. Even as a kid, my father was an excellent swimmer who spent countless hours swimming and diving under the bridge that connected two countries, the USA and Canada. One of his boasts in life was that he had swam across the river as a young boy. I grew up in an Army Camp with a persistent father who made sure his children knew how to swim, and the camp's Olympic-sized pool provided the means to learn early.

The pool was sectioned off from a fenced-off wading area for toddlers connected by a three-foot area for beginners. The largest swimming area of the pool was at the deepest end to accommodate high diving board, with a smaller, shorter board underneath closer to the water. The deepest end of the pool eventually levelled off at the opposite end, with a depth of six feet, roped off to hold the young swimmers not old enough to play at the deepest end. No matter how good of a swimmer, you had to be seven years of age before being allowed on the other side of the rope. Although, it was common for many of us to sneak under it simply by swimming underwater without being caught by the lifeguard.

It was a lovely summer activity for the kids in the camp, and being a strong swimmer, I was one of those kids who were tempted to swim under the ropes to bask in the cradle of water at the deep end. There were so many '*if only*' moments behind the rope watching my brother, who could jump and dive off the boards at the deepest part of the pool. I so wanted to have the chance to jump off that high diving board. Despite the temptation, I wouldn't say I liked to upset the lifeguard, especially as most of the time, it was my dad.

I loved the wonderful feeling of freedom that filled the senses while swimming, especially underwater. Sometimes, it felt so much like home that I was sure breathing would be a breeze, having to remind myself not to attempt it until an unforgettable moment left me in no doubt. One day, I had built enough confidence and convinced the other lifeguard that I was ready. He made a deal with me that since he had watched me several times swimming the width underwater, I would need to prove I was good with swimming strokes on top of the water, and if I could swim across and back without stopping to rest, I would be allowed to swim in the deep end. He had a deal! This test would be a doddle because it was my father who had taught me how to swim.

After quickly passing, I eagerly ran about mid-way to the deeper end and jumped close to the side edge of the pool. I first wanted to see if I could touch the bottom near the edge and found that I could manage it with my toes touching and the water coming to the top of my lip. A few of my friends gathered by the edge, happy to see that I could join them. In their excitement, they proceeded to dunk my head underwater as part of a not well-thought-out initiation ritual for making it to the deep end. Unfortunately, they would lean over the edge whenever I came up for air and push my head back under before I could get some air. All I could manage was gulps of water. I do not know how many times this happened until things went blank. The last thing I remembered was seeing my brother running along the side, yelling at my friends while trying to get to me. The next thing I knew, I was lying on my stomach along the side of the pool with the lifeguard pushing against my back and strangely lifting my arms as I was coughing and spitting out water.

I was soon okay, and as I sat up, I was told that I had to return to the rope side of the pool because I was not yet ready. I was miffed at this outcome because, as far as I was concerned, it was not my fault. However, I would swallow my disappointment after being reminded that I could easily have stayed underwater and swam away from the edge to escape the exuberant play of others. It made sense. My swimming was not the problem; my thinking maturity needed to be prepared.

It was not long before I gave in to the temptation and crossed under the ropes to freedom, although from that time on, after my days of sneaking under the ropes, I would always dive away from the edge. Although I was sure the lifeguard saw me, he let me stay without any reminders. I was thrilled that I had the chance to jump and dive off the diving boards by the end of that summer. I was so proud that I had made it before the designated age limit, and although my father never told me, I was sure he was also impressed.

One meaningful experience occurred after jumping off the high board while enjoying myself exploring the bottom of the deepest part of the pool. While swimming underwater, I completely forgot where I was. For a moment, the sensation of the water on my body felt so familiar, as if I belonged there. I became lost in the familiarity of it all, and I had it in my mind that I could breathe while still under the water. Of course, I was immediately shaken out of my delusion, as I found myself quickly rising to the surface with a horrible burning sensation in my nose and throat. I had to immediately swim to the pool's edge and pull myself out to catch my breath and feel normal again. Not so surprisingly, it was a difficult task dealing with the horrible things happening in my head, along with my confusion about why I would do such a thing in the first place. A tremendous lesson was learned that time around!

LOST IN THE WAVES

My love of water continued over the years, and I was thrilled when my family once again lived close to the city where I was born. We lived just a short distance from the lake, about a mile from our house, which was located on the city's outskirts. Not long after moving back into the area, one sweltering summer evening, my brother and I took a hike down the road, heading towards the beach to cool off. By the time we reached our destination, we had found the beach shoreline empty, but that did not matter; we were determined to cool off by enjoying a good swim in the lake. There were a few waves, but not too forceful, so it took only a short time before we swam further out to avoid them. We were completely absorbed in our thoughts as we floated further and further away from the shoreline.

    We both were so used to swimming in calm waters, having learned to swim in a pool setting and felt the need to go out further to achieve the feeling of swimming without being able to touch the bottom. For some unknown reason, it felt awkward closer to shore, cooling off while splashing and frolicking in the waves. It was time to return after swimming for about one-half hour, caressed by the water's movement and the exhilarating sense of freedom it gave. I felt I could have stayed in that blissful state forever; however, my brother thought it best to return to shore as the waves seemed to strengthen and gather more power by the minute. Being the more robust and faster swimmer, he was always in front, and I am sure he wanted to prove that he could beat me to shore. The race was on!

The closer we got to the shoreline, the stronger the waves, and it was clear that we would be facing a very heavy undertow. By the time we came closer to the shore, I was exhausted, and my energy was weakening just as the waves and undertows were getting stronger. My brother, happy that he beat me, headed across the beach quickly, racing up the incline towards the road, thinking I was right behind him. However, at that time, I could only wish that my whereabouts were precisely where he thought.

I found myself in difficulty, trying desperately to get up after a wave would push me forward. I frantically tried to catch a breath, only to be pulled back again by the now powerful undertow. I had never before experienced such power while being dragged back over and over. It was becoming quite a fighting dilemma. The shoreline was getting further away as I tried yelling for help, but my dear brother could not hear me because of the waves pounding on the shoreline. I was unsure how long I could hold out in this battle with the waves. Before giving up, my brother finally turned to see where I was. I could see his ashen face as he realized I was still in the water, fighting for my life.

It had been quite some time since I had seen him run so fast, and thankfully, he made it in time, as I was sure the next wave would have finished me off. I had no more strength to fight and was about to give up on what I knew was coming with the next undertow movement. Of course, the first words from my brother as he pulled me out of my predicament were, "*Why didn't you say you needed help?*" At that very moment, I did not doubt that he knew, that I learned firsthand that he was in the wrong, knowing that one should never swim alone for the very reason of what had almost happened. This experience for both of us was ample proof of just such caution. At least now, we both became more fully aware that never again would we take for granted any swimming partner's whereabouts. Loving the water as we both did is not enough to keep one safe, and there are no guarantees that being a good swimmer will prevent one from meeting their end. Such was the lesson we learned that day.

Story Reflection

Keeping this story in mind, I am reminded of a quote about water from one of our world's greatest nature lovers, <u>Margaret Atwood</u>. It goes as follows.

> *"Water does not resist. Water flows. When you plunge your hand into it, all you feel is a caress. Water is not a solid wall; it will not stop you. But water always goes where it wants to go, and nothing in the end can stand against it. Water is patient. Dripping water wears away a stone. Remember that, my child. Remember, you are half water. If you can't go through an obstacle, go around it. Water does."*

This quote from Margaret Atwood resonates deeply with me, as it encapsulates the power and patience of water and the lessons it can teach us about life and resilience.

ROUGH RIDE IN RAPIDS

"Nothing is softer or more flexible than water,

yet nothing can resist it."

– Lao Tzu.

I could hardly believe that I was about to embark on a trip down the river in a raft. I can't say it was something on my 'bucket list' of things to accomplish throughout this life journey, but I could scratch it off as just such an experience. As one of the youth leaders of a church group, I had the chance to accompany a group of young adults to whitewater rafting down the Ottawa River. I loved the water, and although I had never attempted such an endeavour before, I had determined that this day's activity would be a lifetime thrill. My husband and I had gone on various retreats with our group, some more demanding of our participation than others. However, this experiential activity would require more demanding hands-on participation versus our usual talking, listening, and observation roles.

I had to admit that most of the rafting experience was delightful. It was a beautiful summer day with blue skies, birds singing and lots of excitement from our group while at the main camp before setting out on our rafts downriver. Everyone was hyper-alert to instructions provided by the rafting company and could hardly wait to board the rafts. We were all geared up with life jackets, and the captain of the raft let us know that his priority was for the raft, not for its occupants. We were on our own if we fell out, although he assured us there were spotters in Kayaks that would help get us to shore if necessary. Once in the raft, it became hard work for me to keep up with the others in our duty as paddlers on the raft, especially when having to keep paddling while going over a rapid. During many of those moments, all one wanted to do was hang on tight to avoid falling out. I had no fear of the water, but my arm strength was something else, proving that it had been quite some time since I had challenged my physical endurance for such an activity. It became self-evident, very quickly, as to why it was so important to sign those waivers before getting into the raft!

Going down the various rapids throughout the river was thrilling and challenging in keeping one's composure as some were more torturous to mind and body than others. However, the peaceful journey between rapids was well worth the hardship and momentary anxiety one endured. I quickly learned firsthand the depth of feeling during an adrenaline rush. Once experienced, I better understood what was meant by addicted to the thrill of an adrenaline rush! We were informed of the last rapid, which would be the most challenging as it was a twenty-five-foot drop. We would need to face this challenge one raft at a time, so we had to wait on a small island close by to wait our turn.

While waiting, we watched in eager anticipation for our turn, and in so doing, we quickly learned that having that privilege was like a two-edged sword. On the one hand, it was great to see what would come as we stood and watched each raft before ours go over the drop, and we were amazed at such an accomplishment. Yet…on the other hand, my mind could hardly understand why anyone would put themselves through such an ordeal and oh my word, what have we got ourselves into? Some in our group were not as eager as others since it looked pretty scary seeing the back end of the rafts flip high in the air. Many in the group with pale white faces just thinking about it gave new meaning to 'seeing one's thoughts.' Not to mention the total look of fear watching the odd person flying out of the raft only to be picked up by one of the Kayaks or carried off by the current at the base of the drop.

The whole situation was more challenging for a few of the guys, my husband being one of them, because they were heavier and more muscular and were told they needed to ride on the back end of the raft to keep the raft from tipping. Instructions were to keep paddling no matter how hard it seemed. The drop, for me, was more accessible, sitting in the middle with the least resistance. I must admit that I was thrilled and, at the same time, relieved that the paddling duty was not as essential in my stable raft position while going over such a long drop. There was much less chance of being thrown out from the middle of the raft. However, even if possible, I was not overly concerned because I did not doubt my ability to swim, and after all, we were all wearing life jackets. If anyone managed to get thrown out of the raft and in trouble, the kayak safety crew was plentiful at the bottom of that particular drop.

The best part of that drop was finding oneself at the bottom right-side-up and still in the raft. Once the raft was out of the way of any that followed, we were told we could jump out of the raft and let the strong current take us to the shoreline, where we would be picked up and given a ride back to base camp for lunch. Now, this was more my speed, and I certainly would love to give myself up to such freedom, especially from 'raft' responsibility and be able to ride the current instead of the rapids. It sounded delightful, requiring no physical exertion as the lifejackets would keep us afloat. Having no more challenging rapids to master, current riding was the way to go! All but one of our group members eagerly jumped out into the water. As for me, I could hardly wait for that magical ride to shore.

Had I known that what was to come would be the most challenging part of my rafting experience, I wonder if I would have jumped out or have been better off staying in the raft in the first place. My exit was more or less sliding off the raft instead of jumping away from it. The raft's edge was at my face when my head popped up. A bit startled, I followed my instinct to dunk back under, thinking the raft would float over me. I had yet to consider the strength and swiftness of the current carrying the folks in the water and the raft at the same speed. I now found myself underwater in the middle underbelly of the raft, going with the flow of the current and the raft at the same time. I could not fight either to come up the other side. I could not beat the current to get in front, so I was in a difficult situation. You could say I was stuck in a bubble that was not in my control. Now, if only that bubble were filled with air! I almost heard my mother saying, *"Well, dear, you seem to be in quite a pickle!"*

At this point, it did not matter how long I could hold my breath, as there was no way it would be long enough to escape my situation. I knew it would do me no good to panic, so if I were to survive, I would need to stay calm and figure out what to do next. I knew the raft captain would not be coming to my rescue as his priority was for the raft. During this part of my predicament, I could feel the life energy slowly ebbing away. Before my body took over and tried to breathe independently, knowing it would not be the answer while submerged underwater, I calmly and firmly spoke to my creator. I said if this was the way I must leave this world, then so be it, and if not, then it was up to him to do something, as I had no strength left to help myself. The strangest part of this crisis was my surprise at how calm I remained throughout it all, and strangely enough, although I did not look forward to it, I thought it was not such a difficult way to go. Of course, I had not yet taken that first breath. My thoughts may have changed at that point.

I did not know how long I remained in what could be described as an almost euphoric state, but suddenly, I popped up on the other side of the raft, coughing and spitting out water from my first massive air intake as I broke free from the water. The captain grabbed my life jacket and pulled me aboard. I remember the sensation of sliding over the edge and into the raft. I felt not a single drop of energy in my whole body, and my first thoughts were, *"This is what a fish must feel like."* I remember my uncle describing big sea fishing and letting the fish tire itself out before reeling it in the boat. I was sure those big fish would have a similar feeling with no energy left to fight what would happen. At that point, I wondered if they, too, felt a need to connect with their creator.

As I lay on the floor of the raft with half of my face submerged in a puddle of water, the group member that had stayed behind in the raft kept telling me to lift my head, stating to me, *"Do you not know that you can drown in that water."* I laughed to myself, thinking that if I did not drown under the raft, then I was pretty sure it was not going to happen with the little puddle of water in the raft. Besides, what had just taken place then and in my previous close encounters with water proved to me that drowning was not the way I would meet my demise. My strength was so weak that it took quite a while before I could even lift my finger. I stayed there until my energy slowly returned, then gradually got up and straddled the raft's edge to enjoy the rest of the rafting excursion, riding along with the current and a little paddling. Life was good, life was beautiful, and I was still alive.

I would have to put this excursion down to a once-in-a-lifetime experience, and my husband begged me never to ask him to go on such an excursion in water again. What can I say? He was not a water lover. I learned through the experience the importance of knowing your strengths and concluded that this type of sport was better left to younger folks. I also felt closer to my creator, knowing that I was in good hands and that when my time was up, I would be okay with it, no matter how that end would come. It was and is essential to go with the flow!

RELAXING IN NATURE

"In every walk with nature, one receives far more than he seeks."

- John Muir

MEMORABLE MOMENTS

Gail's Recollections

So many memorable moments were spent at our lake property high in the BC Mountains, surrounded by nature at its finest. I hold many cherished memories of the many hours spent helping clear and prepare a parcel of land in our chosen part of the wilderness. They were precious times filled with numerous exciting interludes with nature, never to be forgotten. The land was purchased by a group of eight that divided it amongst those who contributed to the group effort. My husband Larry was one of the group members whose intention was to develop his little

parcel of land to become a home away from home and to eventually retire and spend our summers in a cabin that he would finally build on the property. However, things abruptly stopped before all our building plans after clearing was implemented. Sadly, Larry did not have a chance to complete his final cabin project due to his unexpected passing. Despite the changes resulting from this tragedy,

I must admit that I have come to appreciate nature more than ever over many years of enjoying our camping adventures in the trailer established as our home away from home, experiencing our unique property together.

One of my favourite downtime activities was relaxing on the deck, breathing in the energy of this property's beauty and wonder. There was never a dull moment watching ducks, cranes, geese, and otters in their natural habitats in and around the little lake that could be seen from all corners of our property. Their interactions with each other were mesmerizing as we sat on our deck chairs, watching their antics during the summer season.

Getting lost in enchantment at any of the moments spent in this wilderness retreat, no matter if working or relaxing, comes quickly to mind. So many times, it seemed that time would often come to a standstill before the realization came that it was bedtime. There was never a sleepless night at our wilderness retreat, and rising with the sun was given. To be truthful, Larry was the early riser, as I have been known to sit up a bit longer into the night working on my cross-stitch projects.

There was an exceptional moment when I became utterly absorbed by the surrounding nature while sitting at our favourite chilling out spot on the deck of what Larry liked to call the cookhouse. Although not considered a full-sized cabin, it was small building where guests could sleep, and it was big enough with a complete set of cupboards and kitchen appliances where all the cooking was done. On one side of the building that looked out on the vast deck were floor-to-ceiling windows with a sliding door. I was enjoying the outdoors, lost in nature, waiting for Larry to return from helping the fellow next door to our property.

One of my most memorable interludes with nature came while  sitting by myself, just soaking up the atmosphere while getting lost in my thoughts of how fortunate I am to have this opportunity of complete relaxation. While bathing in the warm sun and lovely atmosphere, I soon became aware of some hummingbirds flitting around as if searching for something. How could it be that I did not notice them before? During this interruption, to my peace, I came to the surprising conclusion that it was my first time seeing these little hummers around these parts. I am at a loss as to how I could have missed them during earlier visits. I found it ever so strange that they were even there as I thought they were city dwellers, not forest birds, so I became intrigued to figure out why they were on my deck, miles away from any town or city. They stayed for a while before flitting off toward our neighbour's property.

After speaking with the neighbour, who showed me his bird feeder setup, I soon understood and decided to follow suit and on my next trip to town I would purchase a hummingbird feeder to hang

on the tree by the deck. My neighbour shared his secret recipe of three-to-one ratio of water and sugar that attracted so many birds to his property. How exciting to set up a similar system. I look forward to such joyful entertainment watching these beautifully coloured birds.

Before too long, as neighbours, we were competing to see who had the most birds visiting our feeders and as it turned out, for some unknown reason, I had more birds coming by that first summer of putting up my feeder. Quite a few more than expected and more than I could handle as the feeder emptied much faster than I could keep up. Those little critters always seemed in a frenzy whenever the feeder was empty and did not seem to mind letting me know, as they would dive bomb me with close-to-my-head flybys whenever I was on the deck. If I didn't know any different, I would think them a bit tipsy!

It was time for another trip next door to see what was happening. My neighbour was more than surprised at the drop in the number of the little hummers that came his way. He mentioned that he was becoming annoyed that he saw fewer birds and suspicious about what I was adding to the feeder to entice them away from his feeder to mine. I told him I had only followed his instruction of a three-to-one ratio. Three cups of sugar to one cup of water. He laughed and said no wonder, as I provided a feeder full of sugar syrup instead of sugar water. I had the ratio backward. I immediately changed the ratio and was able to relax once more enjoying my peaceful bird-watching time without being at the beck and call of addictive birds. However, I did notice that this neighbour always had a few more bird visits and wondered if he secretly added more sugar to his mixture. Now, it was my turn to laugh as I knew that if so, he would find himself busy trying to keep up with the demand of their sweet appetites.

It was not too long afterwards after a most delightful day of birdwatching while sitting quietly on the deck, when a couple of the little hummingbirds approached me as if trying to tell me something. Never had hovered so close that I felt I could reach out and touch them. I would need clarification as the feeder was still half full, having been filled a few days earlier. Another trip next door was in order, so off I trotted to inquire if I needed to include something. I was informed that the birds do not like outdated sugar water. These hummers seem to find that it goes stale, and to hang about longer would require 'feeder freshness.' Frankly, I thought they were becoming quite fussy, but because I enjoyed them so much, I made sure it was changed every day, at least when I was at the property from then on.

I did check it out a couple of times to see if the little hummers would keep me informed, and sure enough, each time I left it for more than a day or two, they would fly right up to my face, making little chattering noises to let me know it was time for a change. It's hard to believe that even birds require a *'good before expiry date.'*

Back home, my feeding setup differs, and I do not have to be as persistent with changing the feeder so often since the little hummers seem less selective than the ones at the lake property. Perhaps the difference is due to being my home birds being thankful for small wonders having to survive closer to busier townsfolk with less time on their hands to cater to a bird's needs. Since city birds not living in a wilder area with more relaxed folks with more time on their hands wanting to enjoy their company, keeps them grateful for what they get. Strangely enough, I would have thought it would be the other way around. A little bit backward, do you not agree?

CHIPMUNK SAFTEY TRAIL

Gail relays another great space of relaxation found on their property in the BC mountains, that afforded the perfect spot to watch the early sunrise by the fire pit, where they spent many an evening sitting around the campfire in the company of family, friends and neighbours. It soon became another favourite pastime during those relaxed days at the property retreat. She goes on to relay that she and her husband, Larry, would often take a break and sit and relax near the campfire area on a couple of benches he had made. It seemed the perfect spot to watch the antics of some chipmunks that had set up homesteading. Since it was a fairly open area, they that a few chipmunks while following a usual trail to get to a tree stump on the other side of the firepit faced a daily challenge to arrive at the stump safe from the eagles that would hang about on the top of the nearby trees. Unfortunately for the most endearing small creatures to us, those eagles found them more of a tasty snack.

Larry had decided to give the little critters a fighting chance and  build a few longer benches to help them run undercover for more extended periods to avoid detection by their natural predators. It was a win-win situation as the benches provided extra sitting space for visitors without folding chairs to the campfires. Once completed, the trail changed enough that the tiny chipmunks could now take advantage of the shelter offered and could be found sprinting from bench to bench, running underneath out of sight of the eagles. Many an hour was spent watching in amusement as they made their way safely home. Because they brought so much pleasure to us during those early mornings, Larry would often put some peanuts under the bench, and we would get a kick out of watching them sitting peacefully under the benches, stuffing their mouth and laughing as their little faces grew larger with their stash.

Gail and Larry would often discuss the option of trying to feed them by hand, knowing that some of the neighbours did so, and understood that they would come right up to them to get treats. However they soon learned that many folks in the area started tossing their peanuts a little closer each time until the little chipmunks eventually came to feed off their hand. Surprisingly enough, it was not unheard of that if a peanut was put in a shirt pocket, the chipmunk would run up one's arm and dive into the pocket to get to it. However, since they were often accompanied by their pet dog and occasionally two pet cats, they did not want to discourage the little chipmunks from using their safety trail. Gail states that they both were content knowing that the little "*Chippys*" found treats on their trail, almost as if by magic.

It had been during these interludes with nature, especially in the setting where Gail had experienced so much of the natural wilderness, that she realized there is so much more to this beautiful world filled with wonder and awe for all that must be shared in this world during the journeys of all life forms. It certainly opens one's eyes to understand better the importance of the interdependence of body and spirit, which could occur between species more often if we open ourselves up to the opportunities that cross our paths. Although their planned retirement agenda did not turn out as expected with the passing of her husband, she remains much more aware and appreciative of the beauty and perfection of nature, no matter where she resides or visits. She says, *"I often wonder if those little creatures who gave us so much pleasure feel the same."*

WILDERNESS WONDER

"Outdoor learning invites us to dance with the rhythms of nature, and in doing so,

we find harmony within ourselves."

– Gabriel Cruz.

Shelly's family-nature connection

Growing up in a country setting certainly played a significant part in forming a lifetime filled with a depth of caring and respect for the world of nature not commonly found in most humans. The daughter of Gail and Larry, Shelly, having roots from such a nature-loving family, surroundings and close family ties, took on the unique role of 'protector' to any creature in need of assistance that crossed her path, which, for some strange reason, took place at the oddest of times. It seemed the wildlife in her surroundings took as much of a liking for her as she had for them. To see Shelly in action, whether manipulating her surroundings with landscaping ideas, with her most exciting interactions finding ways to keep critters safe, along with her love for nature, leaves no doubt about the philosophy of a unique energy connection between all species of life that cross a most delightful path.

Shelly recounts memories of visits by her grandmother and the time they spent walking throughout the country property where she spent most of her growing up years. Her grandmother, having a strong love of the outdoors and a most acute eye for detail, would point out unusual and distinguishing signs of nature around the farm that most would miss. Shelly relates that she spent many hours sitting beside her grandmother and reading nature stories worldwide. Based on what she learned from her grandmother, mother, and father, in her mind, all of nature presents the perfect setting for finding what is necessary for humans from all walks of life.

Once a person's eyes are opened to understanding the benefits of so many aspects of the beauty of nature that surrounds us, and finding it the source of our food, entertainment and service to make the life of humans easier. This door of appreciation cannot easily be closed. Those special memories over a lifetime provide beauty and interest for both heart and soul and, without any doubt, reinforce humankind's strong connection with nature. As far as Shelly and her grandmother are concerned, all animals, including the small critters of this world, are like family and deserve excellent care and respect for all they offer those who take the time to observe what is unconditionally offered. Because of many precious memories while growing up, Shelly desires to travel and see some of the wonders that brought so much pleasure from those books of nature. Her attention to detail often demonstrates a love and respect for all things nature, no matter where life takes her.

Shelly relays a few of the treasured interludes with nature from the memories that moulded her heart and mind with such deep respect and affinity for the world of nature and all its splendours. She feels strongly that her interest in all things stemming from nature is indeed part of her heritage passed down to her, especially from her father. It seemed his heart, too, was filled with wonder for the small and sometimes helpless creatures of this world, and he would do his best to keep a close eye on helping wherever he could to bring them out of human harm's way. He was known in his community as a lover of animals and would go out of his way to protect any animal he found needing a helping hand. His rare attention and care from a country farming perspective were easily detectable, such as when he closed off part of his property for the time needed for hatching eggs by a bird that built its nest on the ground in the middle of the driveway. Fortunately for the rest of the family and visitors, there were alternative ways to enter the property, as the driveway had two entrance points. His makeshift protection barriers did not come down until those birds could fly. Luckily, they lived on a corner lot. Whenever he found an animal on the side of the road that had been hit by a car, after careful inspection, he would take it to a taxidermist so that its beauty could be observed even after death. He owned some lovely stuffed animals, such as a red fox, a badger, a baby black bear and a magnificent specimen of an adult white owl. There did come a time, however, when Shelly's mother had to stop the accumulation of stuffed animals, as the house could only hold so many!

Her dad had been an artful landscaper who liked to work with what he found in nature to bring a sense of tranquillity to his work. He loved the outdoors so much that he would often be found out in the fields, exploring ways to avoid hurting the smaller creatures that others found most irritating, especially while working on his farm acreage. Shelly relates that her father would go out of his way to find solutions to share space with critters who were unwelcome on many surrounding properties because of the nuisance factor. As one can imagine, out in the country, this was especially true with skunks, foxes and badgers. Yet, he instinctively knew they were also beneficial to humans as they are known to destroy rats and mice that commonly infest and cause havoc in farm buildings. Although he owed a rifle, he would only use it to scare off most pesty critters versus kill them.

Following his philosophy that *"there is a reason for all creatures, both great and small,"* keeping skunks safe and alive was his way of saying thanks for all they do for us, considering they are such efficient hunters of rats, mice, and other destructive vermin and still be determined to keep the family pets safe and sound. Despite the odours he would need to endure while working, he allowed a family den of newborn kits to live under his work shed. Luckily, his shed was away from the house and family pets, allowing a safe spot for the young kits when the mother was out hunting in the opposite direction close to the small creek that ran through his property. An ideal sanctuary in his mind that was much closer to where he could keep an eye on them. It turned out to be more like a 'spiritual' retreat where he spent many hours creating something useful for the farm or just making some old, forgotten articles come back to life. No matter the object, whether an old, beaten-up bench or chair or restoring an old car, it deserves tender, loving care.

Even though this same mother skunk residing under the shed would often be found rooting around the neighbour's chicken coup in search of eggs, Shelly's father believed there was room in this world for them all. He persuaded the neighbours to let it be as long as no real damage was done. Regarding her connection with this same skunk, this inherited care for animals seemed to spill over from father to daughter. She often saw it walking along the road while driving home from work. Their journeys coincided since the small 'critter' was indeed heading home to its under-the-shed den after completing its mission, after visiting the neighbour's property. Just like her dad, Shelly could only hope that no real harm was done during those neighbourhood visits.

Shelly moved her car slowly with her window rolled down to chat with the skunk. Her father had warned her that such action might not work well for her if she or the skunk felt frightened. However, she was sure she would not be sprayed while praising the skunk for the joy she felt watching its comings and goings from the shed, especially when rounding up her little ones to return to the underground retreat. In these 'close to nature' moments of conversation, she felt obliged to warn the skunk to be careful and not to annoy the neighbours too much. For whatever reason, a connection had been established between the two. She had no fear and, strangely enough, knew that the animal was fully aware there was nothing to be afraid of from her.

As it turned out, the saga of her skunk, who had become more like a companion on the last leg of coming home, did not do so well with the neighbours, who unfortunately were running out of patience, not to mention retaining a different view regarding the wild creatures of nature, not feeling so inclined to be friendly or accommodating to its needs. Of course, they had a legitimate concern for their chickens and the stealing of eggs. The skunk in question was eventually trapped by them and moved to another location. However, it soon returned and settled into the same routine. The neighbours felt something had to be done, and the skunk met its demise with the next visit. To Shelly's dismay, it had been poisoned!

Shelly was heartbroken, knowing the creature was a mother with a batch of 'kits' left behind under the shed, not yet ready to fend for themselves. They still needed to be looked after and fed. Of course, you guessed it. Shelly became the primary provider, feeding them cat food until they were big enough to care for themselves. It could be said that perhaps in some strange way, that mother skunk knew that this travelling home companion, even if coming from the unpredictable human species, would step up and look after her little ones. Whether consciously or not, it has always been understood that an unspoken vibrational energy connection passes from one species to another. If that is the case, then this story speaks to the truthfulness of such an understanding.

Shelly's father worked on the farm by raising cattle for a time, but due to an unfortunate cattle disease that spread through the area, he had to give the endeavour up. He later sold off some acreage and went to work at a landscaping business. His natural talent and a keen eye for detail soon put him in high demand, and he could keep his property in a pristine condition that became the envy of his neighbours. He naturally could make the most of all the beauty of nature with a natural and uncanny ability of tree trimming, planting, and use of foliage and rocks that made the areas he worked on most pleasing to all who viewed its splendour. His talent was not missed when he set his hand to clear a plot of land high in the BC mountains in preparation for a unique retirement spot. No matter where, when he put his heart, hands and spirit to work, he left a distinguishing mark of loving care and attention.

If only they could speak, many of the small creatures of the area could attest to the efforts of Shelly's father, as demonstrated in the previous story about a safety trail for chipmunks. This talent of his, whether landscaping or caring for the animals found in nature, was passed down to his daughter, evidenced by the love and care she took for the homes she would live in, renovating in such a manner that the outdoors was a sight to behold showing the importance of nature and especially her unique retreat high in the mountains of Arizona with all the little touches made to watch nature in all its splendour.

Rescuing animals seems to follow Shelly's journey, as she relates a time of running through a raspberry bush to save a small duck from being attacked by a couple of cats. Her neighbours had made a pond in their yard for ducks that would pass by on their way to wherever ducks go at various times throughout the year. One of those times, a rare duck not often found in the Calgary area landed and rested in the pond. After getting too close to the edge, two of the neighbour's cats spotted it and managed to capture the smaller-than-usual duck.

Fortunately for the duck, Shelly had been drawn to visit at the exact time, witnessing the kidnapping and possible demise of such a rare creature. With no hesitation or worry about the results of such a rescue gesture, she dove into the prickly bush to save the duck, returning it to the safety of the pond. She, of course, was wounded with all the scratches on her arms! Was it pure luck that she was there to rescue..., or was it something else? Satisfaction swelled as she could now watch it fly away after resting up. She found out later about the rarity of this type of duck being spotted in the area, leaving her to feel even more joy in seeing and being part of the life journey of such a rare bird.

Another time, when finding herself at *the right place at the right time,*' Shelly had a critical role in an exciting interlude with nature by saving a baby owl from seagulls. It seems that the affinity she felt was something that not only brought solace to her heart but also could be considered a great benefit for the recipient of such tender love and care. During this interlude, Shelly was going home from work at the Wharf in Vancouver. It had been a busy day, and while enjoying a leisurely walk home, an uncommon commotion a short distance away caught her eye. To her total dismay, she found herself witnessing seagulls that had surrounded a baby owl and had begun an attack that could not be stopped by the distressed mother owl seen a short distance away. The mother owl could do nothing else for her offspring and flew away, leaving the little one at the mercy of the gulls. It would need to succumb to what is often seen as *'the cruelty of nature,'* well understood to us all as *'the survival of the fittest,'* especially in this case of being so outnumbered by the gulls.

On the other hand, Shelly was determined for a different outcome, and feeling a considerable tug at her heart, she ran directly towards the commotion, meeting the gulls head-on with no thought for her safety. She was confident then that the instinctive protective energy that preceded her could have scared off a pack of wolves! She managed to scoop up the little bird and run to find safety for her and the bird. As she finally found some shelter, escaping from the more aggressive seagulls in hot pursuit, she wondered why the other bystanders of what took place did not rush in to help. Because of her quick thinking, she kept the little one from further harm by delivering it to a shelter for wild birds. After the little one was inspected for injuries and found okay, they agreed to keep the owl until it could fend for itself and was big enough to be set free.

Although missing her father greatly after he was killed in a road accident, Shelly is delighted that his genes live on in her as she can easily take on landscaping with the same sense of hard work and enthusiasm that he displayed. Shelly explained that despite her grief, she often feels him close, especially when she sees hawks soaring high in the sky. She appreciated his love for animals, especially birds of all kinds, and rejoiced in his role in passing on such a unique sense of connection to all things found in nature. She keeps his treasured stuffed owl safe from the elements in a glass case, providing ample opportunities to share her father's love of nature with others whenever they view the beautiful creature. He found the owl had met its demise after being hit by a car. He could not just leave it by the side of the road to rot, so he had it stuffed to display the majesty of this once-living creature to others.

How fortunate for those privileged to hear some of her adventures with the *'wild and unpredictable side'* of nature, leaving one to wonder if some folks do indeed have a special calling on this earthly journey to go the extra mile, bringing heart and soul to their sharing experience with nature. At least in Shelly's case, it certainly seems to be the case.

A WALK WITH NATURE

Photos and writing by Irma Paredes Evoli

Wasaga Beach – Nov 13, 2023

Singing Love, Peace, and Harmony in this precious space

Seeing a heart ... the shades of grey off the light blue...with so much light in between and behind...
Endless movements ...
Endless points of connections and distances ...
Moving ... appearing and disappearing...

A rapture of joy I feel within my soul...
What a gift to witness their existence...

I dwell inside the sounds of the wind ...

A world of sounds ... energy... vibrations moving throughout this landscape of 'trees,'
Light and the sky... I see their dance ...

There is infinite LOVE flowing throughout this land ... here and over there ... where you are ...

Dance and Breathe ...

SURPRISING NATURE CONNECTIONS

"Those who contemplate the beauty of the earth find reserves of strength that will endure as long as life lasts. There is something infinitely healing in the repeated refrains of nature – the assurance that dawn comes after night and spring after winter."

- Rachel Carson.

EMOTIONAL WEATHER LINK

"In the vast expanse of nature, we find solace for the soul

and nourishment for the mind."

– Gabriel Cruz.

Robyn's Passage Through Uncertainty

What a magnificent place to reside and bring up a family! Living in British Columbia brings one as close to heaven as humanly possible, at least for anyone feeling as connected to nature as I have felt since our arrival. Over the time we have lived in this area, no matter the weather and how I think, getting lost in the beautiful energy that comes from all aspects of what nature brings soothes my soul in such a way that it is difficult to put into words.

Being that my husband Mark is a career man in the military means we have had to move several times over the years. We have experienced not only excitement but various levels of apprehension, having to adjust to entirely different surroundings with each change in environment. There has always been much to explore with the newness of it all, including new friends, house, and community. Although it is not unusual to go through some difficulties at the beginning of the interactive moving stage throughout the comings and goings in our daily lives, we have always found that we adjust quickly, making the most of what we are presented with each of our moves. With this move, adjustment was quick and easy, and I must admit that my interest in photography peaked when we were stationed here on Vancouver Island. It seemed like an explosion of creative wonder no matter where we ventured in our little area of the world. I was thrilled to be here with our young son and excited with another child on the way.

We hoped for a baby girl to balance out our little family group. Nothing could affect our enthusiasm despite the adjustments we had to face at the time of year of our arrival to this corner of the world. We soon learned that this hemisphere area becomes darker, with less sunlight to brighten our days. The forecast would involve rain or fog daily, which could quickly dampen one's mood during the dreary winter days that often last for months. It was good that I loved every aspect of nature, including the weather. I believe beauty remains in all kinds of weather, no matter the circumstances. One only needs to have an open heart and mind to see the wonder of it all right in front of you, and if possible, take a picture, and you will undoubtedly understand what I mean. I found it reasonably easy to handle until a specific time in my pregnancy when my body and emotions felt out of sync with what I have become accustomed to as my natural happy state of mind.

This was a planned pregnancy, and due to our great desire to have a girl, we could hardly wait to find out the sex of the baby from medical professionals here in BC. However, our hopes were dashed as we discovered that information was unavailable in this neck of the woods. For some strange reason, this news, along with a sense of fear and anxiety for our unborn baby, took a strange hold over me at this particular time. Perhaps my feelings were triggered by the dreariness of the weather, but whatever the reason, it left me uneasy about the pregnancy. I did not know if there was something wrong either with my ability to carry or with the baby, but something was not right. Within a short period, I started to feel desperate in search of something, anything to change the dark, negative, unsettling feelings that were slowly taking over.

A friend of mine had recommended Reiki to help me become more relaxed and help bring balance to my emotions, and at that point, I thought, great, I was ready to try anything to put my heart, body, and mind at ease. It felt so strange that as the weather became heavier and duller, which had never bothered me before, now seemed to lower my spirits each day. Since I felt so attuned to nature after our arrival, could this miserable weather be trying to tell me something? Did this mean the weather would control my feelings and emotions from that time forward? Admittingly, it will need to remain a mystery to me how something so wonderous as the beauty found in nature could have such an impact on me and what was taking place.

What was happening in this world, especially when I was in the process of setting a reiki appointment? It seemed the most sensible thing to do once becoming aware of such a terrible nightmare. I do not usually remember my dreams or nightmares when I wake in the mornings. However, ready or not, this nightmare's revelation would not be quickly forgotten. The clarity of it stayed forever as if it had just happened yesterday. It was seen as a nightmare of something dark and evil that may harm the unborn baby, leaving feelings of being terrified! All through the night, the battle continued, fighting for the life of her unborn child. I remember yelling, *"You are not having my baby!"* Thankfully, during this nightmare battle, I won, and the dark, evil shape disappeared. I awoke the next morning feeling great relief, joy, and excitement for my growing baby belly.

I knew my baby was safe just as the rain finally stopped, giving in to marvellous sunlight shining down to brighten the days. All the negative feelings dissipated with the coming brightness. Although I often wondered if the weather was responsible for what had happened or if it was something completely different, I know that sunshine played a significant role in lifting my spirits. Not long after that terrible night, I recall stepping out of the shower into the sun shining bright through our bathroom skylight. I stood silent in the middle of sunbeams streaming over my body, and in that magical moment, with unimaginable joy, I looked down at my now big baby belly, glowing pink. I could hardly hold back the tears of relief knowing I would have a beautiful baby girl. My love and appreciation for all that nature brings to our wonderful world returned in full force. I knew those dull and dreary days that come every winter would never again overtake joyful feelings; to this day, it has remained so! Since then, I have snapped some lovely photos of our surrounding area on this beautiful island, especially during winter, proving that all is truly well in my world!

A NATURE WALK INTERRUPTION

Mark & Robyn's Dog Walk

Living in the Comox Valley, surrounded by so many magnificent views of nature, brings more pleasure than can be expected in a lifetime. One is left feeling privileged with untold unexpected opportunities to interact with nature in ways that can be unbelievably comical or awe-inspiring. It is truly a paradise for anyone wanting to use their camera fully. It matters not whether one is a professional photographer or an amateur who loves to capture many of nature's wonders on film. Their photos will not only be inspiring but also tell a story. It is guaranteed that opportunities will pop up least expected.

The area where we live has a large population of deer. Warning signs line the streets all around town, and whether walking or riding a bike, one only has to travel a short distance before observing a sign to be extra careful and cautious. It is not unusual to pass a deer busily munching on grass or blackberries while you walk about, taking in this place's unique ambiance. Most often, it will just look up at you and continue chewing.

I remember one lovely sunny spring day when Mark and I walked our dog, Poppy, through the woods. All three of us had thoroughly enjoyed walking a trail through the forest foliage and watching Poppy explore all she could while following alongside us. The air was fresh, and our spirits were elevated from our walk. We had just come out of the woods and noticed something entirely unexpected as we were about to return to our car. Out of the forest suddenly appears a deer followed by her little fawn.

This mama deer looked our way, quickly crossed the road, and hopped over the ditch and into the bush. Her fawn was following close behind until it caught sight of Poppy. Sometimes, a fawn's curiosity is more vital than instinct to keep close to mom because the wee fawn just turned and came leaping down the road to see our dog. Whatever was taking place, we were in the right place at the right time, watching in amusement as the two stood nose-to-nose for some time. Poppy's curiosity matched the little fawn's interest, giving us a rare moment in nature.

It's funny that no matter how many signs you see, it is always surprising to catch sight of so many of nature's wilderness animals up close and personal, bringing a spark of glee to one's heart for having the opportunity. And what a sight to behold, watching Poppy's tail standing at first straight up in the air one minute and the next, wagging like crazy with her nose busy sniffing the little fawn. For those precious moments, time stood still, although I am not so sure the mother dear was as calm and serene about the situation. It is hard to say just how long those moments stretched. Still, the scene before us opened our hearts to a place of love and energy connection within the bounds of nature as we looked on in amazement at the explorations of curiosity and the mama deer who cautiously stood in the bush watching and waiting for her fawn to join her.

After a while, it seemed the little fawn's curiosity was satisfied, and the connection was broken as it turned and quickly leapt down the road. Watching it ever so gracefully fly over the ditch to catch up with her mom was beautiful. We managed to keep Poppy at bay as the fawn ran off because Poppy was all set to play for a bit longer, wanting to run with it. Our rambunctious pet wasn't done. It was good that the little fawn left, as Poppy's play would have been too much for the delicate and fragile-looking fawn. How fortunate that I had my camera ready and got a few snaps of what happened. It will remain a treasured experience for us to remember in fondness that special day of interruption while coming out of the woods.

The whole incident made me think that it would be good to have some writing on the backside of the signs as a special warning for nature to be careful of unexpected humans crossing their trail.

UNEXPECTED ENCOUNTER

"Outdoor learning invites us to dance with the rhythms of nature, and in doing so,

we find harmony within ourselves."

- Gabriel Cruz.

Cousin Brian's Wilderness Treasure

This unique nature story comes from my cousin Brian, who was born and raised in a small city in southern Ontario and found that exploring or experiencing nature's wilderness animals was limited to what is seen on TV nature shows or trips to the zoo. Since his earliest memories, Brian has been keen to see more of nature and its wild animals in their natural habitat. How disappointing it must have been that instead of being unable to experience the wildness of the deep forests up close and personal, his wilderness interest would need to remain in the realms of wishful thinking. As life progressed, at least in his youth, this wish was put aside to make room for other life commitments that often take precedence over exploring dreams and possibilities that seem far out of reach.

During those early years of growing up to adulthood, he recalled the many times he had gone on trips with his family to visit relatives in northern Ontario. He would revel in unique and exciting stories his uncles and cousins told. Those stories were filled with incidents with some of the wilder species of animals found in the bush areas close to where they lived. They would often discuss all the wilderness wonders they had seen during their outings and treks through the forests. Of course, hunting deer was high on the list. While hunting, they often caught sight of the odd wild animal a short distance away, yet they had experienced more interludes with birds of prey, rabbits, and other smaller animals of the forest up close. Although not overly interested in hunting, Brian could only dream of such adventures, especially as the odd coyote was the wildest thing he knew of from his surroundings. Even then, he has yet to observe one himself.

Listening to the stories always left him feeling a bit left out, not having anything to tell that would match the wild and woolly adventure stories his cousins would relay about living in the wilderness country. Because of not living in the same type of setting other than staying for short family visits, the chances were slim to none of fulfilling nature's wilderness treasures, and as it turned out, the fewer chances of fulfillment, the stronger the desire. Although he deeply desired to see or experience something similar in a wilderness setting in his early youth, this exploring nature desire would remain in the 'if only' field of thinking and, as time passed, took a lesser place in his heart and mind. He thought that perhaps one day, when he was old enough to become independent and explore more of the world on his terms, this desire to see more of the world of nature would be rekindled.

Once he started to work in the refinery plants in the area where he lived, he was able to take advantage of working out of town. Since many of the out-of-town journeys were in the country's northern regions, his old familiar desire to experience the wild treasures of nature began to surface, especially when the time arrived with an opportunity to travel to the Oil Sands in Alberta. The refinery plant was located at Fort McMurray, deep in the heart of the wilderness. Knowing this perked up his past wilderness desires of youth, and if ever there was a chance to experience the treasures found in the deep forests, this job experience was his chance. He was looking forward to the excitement of sharing some up-close and personal stories to tell on his next visit with northern relatives. Brian related that the sleeping and eating quarters of the camp were situated deep in the heavy bush territory and a fair bit from the nearest town; hence, the routine of travel to and from work was by bus. Some of the construction crew did have cars, so there would be an odd trip to town, but for the most part, a significant part of travel time was between two main camps.

For this job site camp, one was made up of the plant executives, and the other camp location farther afield was for the construction workers. Between these two main camps was a desolate roadway of about one and one-half miles. Entertainment for the workers would occur at the executive camp where the bar was located. They often head out to the camp after supper for a drink or two. Now, the road to the bar was relatively isolated and more of a trail-like driving roadway. Although caution was given, walking to and from the camps was possible. Yet at the same time, we were discouraged from hiking the trail road after dark in such a wilderness setting. Anyone doing so would be taking quite a chance of meeting up with some unexpected wildlife, such as black bears and wolves, leaving no safety guarantees. Not knowing how things would turn out or if anyone could come to the rescue soon enough impacted any desire to take that route, despite his longing to see some wildlife up close and personal. Brian was not a risk-taker and could curtail his desire to take over and head out on foot to meet any wild animals head-on. Although walking in a group worked well, keeping with the safety in numbers theory on the way to the bar and driving back became the norm. For him, being a city boy at heart, most outings were safely taken in his construction buddy's car. Better to be safe than sorry was the motto!

The trip between camp and the refinery plant took place by bus, a perfect way to safely see and experience some of the unique wilderness. Brian recalled a time when the bus was delayed while some black bears were checking out the dumpster cuisine from the campers' leftovers, and the bus had to wait for some forestry folks to come and chase the bears before the bus could continue. Of course, a few workers took advantage of the situation and stepped off the bus to get a few photos of the bears. They were warned, however, that if they did not return to the bus right away, they were in jeopardy of losing their jobs. Passenger safety was a priority for the bus driver, who would be held responsible if anything happened to any workers on the way to or from work.

As it turned out, during many of these bus rides, opportunities popped up occasionally, allowing some exciting views of smaller wildlife treasures, such as foxes and other small animals lurking in the bushes on the way. The closer to the plant, the more likely it is to see foxes as they were camping in underground dens under the warm pipes. Due to the harsher weather in the far north, warm pipes were the perfect place for many litters of foxes. The younger ones were so cute, and tossing out food soon became the thing to do for some of the workers. Brian relates that when the workers made up their lunches, they would pack a bit extra to have something to toss out for the cute little kits or cubs, depending on what they liked to call them. It had become quite a sight for Brian and the rest of the crew to watch these little ones come running out as soon as they saw the bus arriving, knowing there would be food waiting for them.

Unfortunately, there always seemed to be a downside as they would soon rely on food provided for them, which would interfere with the natural order of things, encouraging more dens that, in turn, could create problems with the refinery pipelines, especially as the fox and litter numbers would become more prominent and more challenging to control due to such easy access to food. The officials had no alternative but to trap and move them farther afield, and if the workers continued to feed them, they would find their way back. The next step would need to be more permanent, so it seemed that the compassion the workers felt in feeding these cute little wild treasures was strongly discouraged. There was always something new to learn about the wilderness and how man's ignorance leading to interference can often disrupt both man and wildlife, despite good intentions. Stop feeding them soon became the order of the day!

Some interesting facts about foxes can be found at https://allthingsfoxes.com/fox-babies/. *Fox babies have a few different names. Some call them kits, some call them cubs, pups, or whelps, and most call them babies. Fox Cubs are the first term used for them, while kits are a newer term. Most fox litters are small, between 1 and 6 kits per litter. However, some species of foxes can have 10+ kits per litter. Arctic foxes have a much larger litter, with fourteen kits or more. This may be due, in part, to the fact that their survival rate is lower, living in extreme winter conditions. This can also be because many arctic foxes are migratory, and migrating animals have a greater mortality rate.*

Seeing the odd elk wander through the refinery was not unusual and always a treat to witness from time to time while at work. Keeping doors closed in the dorm trailers at camp was essential because the odd black bear would periodically drop by. To them, an open door was an invitation to pay a visit to the individual sleeping quarters to sniff out any snacks or treats that happened to be lying around. Although Brian had never witnessed this happening while he was at the camp, he had heard from others that it was not a pleasant experience since a bear can make quite a mess of one's belongings in search of food. Because the camps were in a forest wilderness, an alarm system was set around the perimeters to prevent the wildlife from interfering or invading. These alarms were made up of sounds of gunshots, which not only surprised any wildlife from entering but also often startled the new influx of workers who were not used to hearing guns blazing. There was always that smarter-than-average bear that could not be fooled, so… keep the doors closed!

Looking back at his experience while working in the northern wilderness of our country, Brian relates that the highlight came during a drive between camps after catching a glimpse of a wolf that turned out to be a mother and her three pups walking along the road. He managed to get the driver to stop so he could get out and take pictures of what they saw. They worked to get relatively close and wanted to take advantage of such an up-close and personal opportunity. As they were snapping photos, the driver called for him to quickly get in the car, pointing out what he spotted across the road. Brian turned to see the piercing eyes of the alpha male just across the road, walking in sync with the mother and pups with a watchful eye on the scene that was a tad too close for comfort for either of them. Luckily, he was close to the car but, at the same time, managed to get a few snapshots of an enormous grey wolf who, if desired, could have made it a bit difficult to reach the car door in time. Now, that experience was more than he could have imagined in his desire to be up close and personal.

Brian had managed to see and live in the wilderness as his wish had come true, including his deep desire to visit and experience some of its untamed animals. This part of his working journey allowed him to fulfill his boyhood dream of a treasured experience to be kept close to his heart and mind for the rest of his days. Not just glimpses of wildlife as the stories told by his cousins, but a very close-up and personal experience of an exceptional wilderness treasure, that of a northern Wolverine family. Just wait until the next visit to his family, and…he had pictures to prove just how close he came to wildlife in their natural habitat. To his mind and the mind of many, Nature never lets us down, so how could it get any better than that?

THE ALLURE OF NATURE

"In every walk with nature, one receives far more than he seeks."

–John Muir.

Arlene's Goat Story

Cartersville, Georgia, is a beautiful place to visit, providing much to ponder when considering stories in all forms of nature. It has terrific sightseeing spots, lovely large homes in woodsy areas, quaint little stores, and shopping areas. However, because the town is surrounded by nature at its finest, one's imagination is quickly filled with wonder and awe at the majesty of woodlands, rivers and mountains within such easy reach, no matter where you find yourself in the area. Having had the chance to view some of what is offered, I was privileged to meet Arlene, who resides in an area with abundant free open spaces and a surplus of beauty found in surrounding woods to keep animals happy and busy.

Having had the chance to see a bit of this area, it is no wonder that it aligns nicely with Arlene's affinity with animals. To her mind, the animals she gathered over the years are part of the family, forming a 'unit of love' that makes her family's life more joyful. She loves to watch and interact with her animals at various stages of development and especially enjoys watching them at play. At the time of the story, her 'family' household also consisted of her husband and daughter, possibly four dogs, one Cockatiel bird, and a cat. Her two horses were housed at a different location. At that time, she was in the habit of bringing home strays or injured or abandoned dogs left on the roadside.

To Arlene's way of thinking, it was the most alluring challenge of service to give help when needed since all things in nature are worthy of love and care, including discarded animals. One of her primary missions was to take them in to become part of the family or find suitable homes that offer tender, loving care and bring them back to health. Her reputation for a kind and compassionate nature towards animals did not go unnoticed, as folks in the area often called upon her for assistance with animals needing a home. If Arlene could not take them in herself, she would not stop until she found what was required for their better good. Her heart goes beyond a mere love for animals. In her life journey, her heart is intertwined closely with nature as a unique demonstration of love for the animals that cross her path.

Now, one must remember that a household can only handle so much, and there came a time when hubby put his foot down and declared..., *'no more.'* It did not take long after this affirmative assertion when Arlene was approached by someone who came across three little goats in desperate need of attention and would require a place to stay. With a heart so big and filled with love for animals, how could one say no to such a plea? With no hesitation, Arlene declared that she would, at the very least, help find them a place to stay. A placement for one of the goats was managed immediately, leaving no alternative but to bring the other two home with her. Her first thought was to let them cozy up with the dogs, and perhaps her husband wouldn't notice; however, that plan was foiled as one of the dear little creatures was not doing so well and needed to come inside for some tender loving care and feeding. Time for plan B!

After explaining the circumstances of the goats to her hubby, he caved and let the little one come inside. One would be hard-pressed to believe the determined one standing his ground with a resolve to limit the animal gathering, as, low and behold, he became the constant caregiver of the weak baby goat. Her husband nursed it back to health until it was ready to mix with the other animals on the outside. One just had to admit that sometimes nature calls out for comfort, and turning your back on such a call would be impossible. It also becomes apparent why the necessity of standing one's ground due to becoming too attached makes it even harder to let go, and there is only so much room in one's home and pocketbook to provide the kind of care necessary for all to remain comfortable.

Arlene managed to find a place for the second goat; however, the little one would remain with them until a safe place could be located. Since getting more accustomed to having it around, it's not all that surprising that it soon became part of the family. This little one loved to frolic and play with the dogs and quickly began to act as if it was part of the dog pack; however, it soon became noticeable that goat's play is a little different than dogs, once witnessing in action that head-buttling. To a young goat, it is a must for maximum enjoyment! Unfortunately, with the steady growth of horns, a concern soon surfaced about an unwanted outcome for the dogs if they had to continuously endure this type of play.

Without exception, it became apparent to Arlene that a mere acceptance to bring all the enjoyment that nature offers into the family is not always the best solution. It was quickly determined, at least in this case, that separation of the species was necessary, primarily through those lively moments of youth. However, one must admit that it was an exciting way to experience such a learning curve, knowing that even animals can have issues with the overexuberance of play. Fortunately for Arlene and her family, a home was found for the adorable little goat. It would be accepted at the same place as its companion. Soon, Arlene's family domain returned to normality despite her husband's  more profound line-in-the-sand message; "*There is no more room at the inn.*" "*And this time…I mean it!*" As you, dear reader, can easily guess, only time can tell.

GOOD DEEDS GONE ASTRAY

"Nature's lessons are timeless, teaching us patience, resilience,

and the beauty of embracing change."

- Gabriel Cruz

Sister Suzie's Clash with Nature

My sister's home environment is a haven for many of the little creatures of nature found in the suburbs. It is not surprising to find nightly visits of raccoons and a family of skunks that have taken up residence under a shed at the side of the house. Of course, the deck also offers a unique retreat for a few possums. Other than the odd spraying incidents whenever one of the dogs gets up close and personal to one of the skunks, no actual harm comes from the animals sharing backyard space. Although no human encounters have taken place, a few traps have been set to catch the skunks, hoping to find them other accommodations. So far, other than a couple, the skunk family seems to be in tack under that shed, so one must learn to put up with those odd moments when that unique skunky aroma drifts in the window, riding on the tail of the gentle night breeze.

When visiting, besides the warm hospitality that greets you on arrival, you soon become lost in the mesmerizing sights and sounds of so many birds, bees, plants, and flowers under the canopy of two giant maple trees surrounding her deck. Relaxing in the shade found on the back patio deck on summer visits gives the impression of being surrounded by a world of nature at your fingertips. What a joy to sit and watch nature at its finest while enjoying a cool drink lounging under the shade of those maple trees. One can spend hours just listening and watching the birds sing out to each other, along with the mischievous squirrels trying to rob those same birds of their treats at the bird feeder. Much pleasure is found in observing the comical antics of the squirrels chasing each other up the trees and running along the top of the fence surrounding the backyard. During those times, one finds it hard-pressed not to smile.

As a frequent visitor, having one's heart and mind filled with healing energy is always a pleasure that brings solace to the soul. Such inviting energy is continually available through visits with sister Suzie and her husband Greg, who have big hearts that welcome all types of nature and humans who arrive for a taste of their hospitality. Fortunately, catching up in the tranquillity of lazy summer days in this environment provides the kind of peace one could only find in the 'Garden of Edan' for a short time, depending on which end of the visiting scale one sits since only the seasonal nature portion stays longer than a week or two. And so, at least for me, no matter the length of stay, coexisting with suburban nature and abundance, although momentarily, seems profoundly moving and much appreciated.

One would presume that the good deeds of this welcoming couple would always bode well, as we suppose all excellent deeds should. However, there can be a downside and, unfortunately, even the odd, ugly moment or two, considering what must happen after a few skunk encounters. Everything was going nicely until one summer when a new chapter in the enchanting environment began, setting the stage for a different scenario that would eventually turn things around. It all started with a visit from the grandkids, who were determined to try and get the squirrels to eat from their hands. Well, of course, the squirrels were willing, with some coaxing, to cooperate. The experiment was considered worthwhile, with everyone finding joy in the endeavour, apart from a slight nip on a finger, but no actual harm was done. A new mission was now genuinely set in motion with the daily feeding of these cute little squirrels.

If one knows anything about squirrels, more is expected to follow once feeding occurs. The grandkids were visiting for a few weeks that summer, so a big bag of peanuts was brought to keep the little critters happy. Part of the fun was to watch the squirrels sitting so calmly while opening the shells to get the prize peanut, which was quickly eaten. It was a great time to catch a photo or two as they busied themselves with their eating task. By the end of their stay, the kids had named each of the growing number of squirrels showing up for the feast. It seemed that the first few squirrels had passed the word on to their friends, and soon, the number had swelled to around six or more, showing up daily. This new feeding dimension added to the tranquil interlude with nature, and it seemed a good idea to continue even after the kids had gone home.

Of course, the squirrels helped enormously with the new transition as they could show up at the patio doors early every morning, looking for nourishment. They like those peanuts! My sister thought cleaning up the shells was not a hefty price for watching the cute eagerness demonstrated when the squirrels arrived for their daily sustenance. Before long, they began to show up at the door more frequently during the day, looking for more and more, especially at the end of the summer during what seemed a frenzy to grab and run to hide the peanuts in chosen easy-access places, stocking up for the winter.

It was relatively easy during the first few years of feeding the little critters. Besides, it was fun to see how close they would come to retrieving the prize while tossing the peanuts closer and closer to the door. The bags of peanuts were shared with the birds, especially the bluejays and cardinals that would show up for a piece of the action. Their peanuts would be tossed to the ground below the deck, allowing them to dive down from the tree and pick them up before any squirrels could get

them. Once the squirrels figured out what was happening, the race was on to see who got there first. One always knew when the birds dropped by for a peanut with their unique sounds, letting you know that they, too, expected a morsel. It did not go unnoticed that the squirrels, over time, were getting braver with letting you know that they had arrived expecting some nourishment, sometimes even tapping on the window of the door or a little scratch on the screen to let you know it was feeding time.

At this point, sister Suzie still managed to feel good about the good Samaritan deed that was taking place. Peanuts were not too expensive, and although they were going through many bags over the spring, summer, and fall, cleaning up the mess on the deck was doable. There was some hesitation with the complete pleasure of this good deed as the digging up of planters took place. Unfortunately, it seemed the perfect place for them to hide that winter stash at the end of summer. However, she had yet to find complete displeasure as the cuteness continued to override an expanding uneasiness that grew along with the bravery and familiarity of what was becoming to be seen as 'pesky' squirrels. Warnings from others were starting to surface. A vague recollection from someone stating that if they managed to get into the house came to mind. Something like possible damage and difficult to catch, so be wary of their friendliness.

It was difficult to understand how something so special as the good feeling of helping nature with a giving heart could turn into a battle of wits. Such a thing happened as those over-zealous, pesky squirrels were now climbing the screen and making a real mess of it all with their sharp claws. A new screen for small animal attacks like squirrels  was now in the works. There was no doubt about the screen needing to be replaced. It almost seemed impossible for such small creatures to cause so much destruction. Not only had they made a mess of the screen, but two of the little devils managed to get in when the door was left open a bit. It seems they managed to do a quick kitchen tour before running back out, scaring the wits out of my soft-hearted sister. Now, they were in real trouble.

Like a declaration of war, they had taken their familiarity too far! Unfortunately, it was not simple breaking the feeding habit, especially for visitors who still thought it a thrill to see the little critters up close and personal. The greed displayed after successfully feeding these small animals over some time gives credence to the description of one of Suzie's friends. *"They are just bushy-tailed rats!"*

Although the feeding ended abruptly, the squirrels continued to hang about the deck near the patio door for a time, just in case. It's funny how they always seemed to be aware when visitors arrived. Perchance, a morsel or two was possible, especially as peanuts were always available on the counter by the door. It was temptation personified by their little brains just waiting for their chance to grab a few. Excellent care with the screen door was now a priority. Unfortunately, just after the new screen was installed, someone succumbed to the endearing look on the other side of the door and threw a couple of peanuts. There  were a few photos of the cute little creatures eating their spoils of war. It was a real shame that the pleasure was so short-lived; that day, a new hole was made in the screen. The end of the feeding saga came with the arrival of two dogs belonging to my sister's son. The pesky squirrels have given up and are back to their original habit of running the fences and trees; the closest they get is the deck railings, providing fewer chances of camera closeup shots. They now seem camera shy, avoiding people altogether, even more so being chased by diligent dogs who protect the household and surrounding deck with their loud barking. They are not overly fond of squirrels, and the feeding expectation is presumed to be wholly diminished once a new generation of squirrels has replaced the pesky mob.

It took a while, but backyard tranquillity once again surrounds my sister with very cautious squirrels not expecting to be fed, at least not from this house in the neighbourhood. The area is filled only with the sights and sounds of peace and back to a beautiful nature-filled ambiance with various plants, flowers and birds to fill the air with tranquil energy. Of course, a few anxious moments of odd sounds are coming from under the deck and shed with nightly visitors. At least now she no longer needs to clean up after those pesky squirrels, although a bit of cleanup persists with the feeding results of those unique calls from the birds getting louder and more frequent. Umm…something to watch closely, wouldn't you think?

MONKEY MISADVENTURE

"We were meant to explore this earth like children do, unhindered by fear, propelled by curiosity and a sense of discovery. Allow yourself to see the world through new eyes and know there are amazing adventures here for you."

- Laurel Bleadon Maffei.

Curtis and Bradley's Adventure Story

This story, which embraces too many lessons to count, took place many years ago on a special outing, encompassing outstanding experiential significance for two very young boys with heads filled with adventure. It all happened while enjoying a day out with their grandparents in a magnificent green-coloured Chevy Nova car. Riding around in their grandparents' car was a delight for both boys, especially for the precocious older boy Curtis, who had an unwavering fascination for cars. On telling the story, he quickly inferred that he remembered being fascinated with the car's unusual green shade, explaining that he was sure it was hand-painted. Curtis considered their ages 7 and 5 or younger. Both boys indicated great pleasure in having had a chance to go out for a car ride in such a fancy car and considered it an adventure on its own, allowing them to explore their new world further. Little did they know it would be a more exciting adventure than anticipated.

The time of this interlude with Nature was in the early 1970s when the area in Florida where their family had settled was in an earlier stage of population and property growth. Due to all the surrounding land clearing and development happening around them, living and growing up during this time, they felt like they too were part of early settlers, exploring new lands and always looking for adventure no matter where it was found. Riding with windows down and the wind blowing across their faces as they watched the rugged world of bush and trees go by seemed the best stimulation to expand adventurous minds in preparation for their subsequent thrilling encounter in nature.

During this outing, they would be stopping by the property of a friend of their grandparents. As the car pulled up the driveway to the house, the boys were told to stay in the car as it would be a quick stop. If they decided they wanted to get out to stretch their legs, they were warned, "**Do not go near the monkey**!" Not much information was given besides that the monkey was a chained-up Chimpanzee. Much later, they learned the need for this breed of monkey to be tied up as there seemed to be very little to do, and the property was surrounded by bush. The monkey owners did not want the chimp to wander off and get lost.

For one uncaged monkey with no companions to occupy its monkey mind, it would seem to any observer that the monkey also needed adventure and would likely appreciate some activity as much as the boys. In the boys' minds, what else could this warning be but a call to more exploration, if only to satisfy curiosity? At least, that is how Curtis interpreted the caution. However, in the grandparents' minds, the monkey being out in the open could only be construed as an open invitation to disaster for anyone with little knowledge of monkeys and their habits, and more so with young, inquisitive minds such as the two boys involved in this tale.

One can only imagine what went through the curious minds of the two boys on hearing there was a monkey nearby! It had to be a summons to high adventure, and not surprisingly, as soon as grandparents were out of sight, that car door flew open, followed by boots quickly hitting the ground and a beeline, heading straight over to the place they were told to avoid for a closer look. With the monkey in sight, their excitement heightened and, in a moment or two, suddenly changed. According to Curtis, his enthusiasm subsided, and they both felt the need to figure out a way to create more excitement for the adventure. Now, this is where the story takes a strange bend, or more of a fork in the journey road, leaving me to relay Bradley's perspective of how they came to the apex of the adventure.

Bradley remembered observing only a chain hanging down from a tree. Admittingly, he was told by his brother that perhaps there was a monkey on the other end. Despite specific agreed-upon details, both boys noticed minimal action since the monkey had been quietly minding its own business, demonstrating no interest in the two boys. What a disappointment with such exciting possibilities only to find three energy beings merely looking at each other. It is hard to pinpoint who came up with the idea of throwing a few pebbles directly at, or close by, the monkey with the simple intention of only getting some active response. However, both admitted to throwing a few to get its attention, although at that first action, little did those boys know what was set into motion. It would not go well for our little adventurers during this monkey altercation.

At the beginning of this 'monkey minds, meeting' when the first few pebbles were thrown, it was determined that a few more pebbles might do the trick since they found no response. Uncertain of the actual culprit, someone thought, why not get a little closer? However, according to Bradley, the idea to get closer came from his older brother Curtis, who he was pretty sure was the one who encouraged him to go and pull the chain to see what would happen. What could be the harm? Especially with so little action coming from the chimpanzee, who seemed unwilling to move, unlike any of the monkeys they had seen before in cages. They figured it should have turned out okay since it was on a chain, and after all, they were free from constraints and able to get away quickly if needed. At least, that was the thinking at the time.

Unbeknownst to the boys, this primate was very much aware of his chain length and had a mind that anything within reach was, in fact, fair game. No matter the details of how it went down, that monkey had been disturbed and not exactly thrilled with the stone toss. Without a moment's notice, within the blink of an eye, as soon as Bradley had stepped across the unknown parameter, that monkey, in one flying leap, ended up close and personal. On a humorous note, it could be construed as a meeting of the minds versus two mischievous boys encouraging some action.

According to Curtis, before he was able to come to the rescue of his little brother, that monkey ran up to Bradley, put him in a headlock and began to lash out, hitting his brother's head. At this point in the tale, according to Bradley, he pulled the chain, and before he knew it, that monkey jumped out of the tree, landing directly on his head. There was nothing else to do but scream for help. All the commotion let the grandparents know they were in trouble. First on the scene was Gramma, who, without any hesitation, went into a flying rage and immediately started into a mode of attack to get the monkey to release the boy from its grip. Of course, to the monkey's surprise, it was now dealing with a much bigger and angrier human. It did not take long to protect itself; it released the boy to fend off a 'mad woman,' leaving it no option but to retreat quickly.

After a quick inspection of the crying boy, he was deemed okay, suffering only from his pride and a few scratches on his head. Now, Curtis, sticking to his story, believes Bradley's head should still show signs of a scar, either from a bite or deep scratch, as he saw blood. Had their grandmother not arrived so quickly…, it bears not thinking of what could have been the result. Of course, he was sure he tried to stop Bradley from such a foolish action, but it was too late. What an adventure that day was, and can you imagine what countless lessons were learned from such an experience, no matter how the event played out? We are unsure if the monkey suffered any scratches or bruising while fending off a furious woman, although you could easily surmise that its pride was also injured.

Now, as we ponder on this adventurous story and the lessons from nature as we come to terms with things out of one's control, especially thinking about the young *monkeying around minds*, not fully understanding or being careful and following the directions of elders, it could be said that experiential learning happens for everyone involved that day, including that monkey. The dangerous mishap of the story could have been avoided in many ways. However, what a way to learn to put more thought into one's actions. Unsure who got the worst of the encounter, the monkey or the boys, especially Bradley, although we can be confident that both faced a traumatic moment despite any version being subject to foggy recollections of the whole incident. At least now, both boys need only be afraid of loose monkeys and not those seen in a cage.

This nature story would need only time and perception to know if it bears out deeply learned lessons, but it does leave us to ponder who should have been locked up. Being human and having the privilege to be part of the natural world shared by all energy beings indeed has consequences for actions. It is hoped that the monkey had a chance to pass such an adventurous story to its relatives, just as it was passed on to this relative of the boys. What would that version look and sound like? One wonders if the chimpanzee also learned an important lesson. Be wary when encountering the enraged energy of human females in protection mode! This whole incident could be seen as a misadventure for them all, including the monkey, and learning through unplanned surprises does indeed take place no matter what end of the encounter you look at.

A STARTLING NOTION

"We do not see nature with our eyes, but
with our understandings and our hearts."

-William Hazlett

Sandra's Childhood Story

The best part of nature for me is animals. I learned so much from them in my early years of growing up. They were not only my friends but very often my teachers about the upsides and downsides of life lessons. Growing up as an only child was lonely. Being alone and feeling isolated was all I knew. In my early childhood, my family considered me timid and tried to protect me the best they knew by sending me to spend time with other family members. Being raised by busy parents, time spent to match me up with another child my age did not happen. I grew up in a neighbourhood without kids my age, so in the early years before school, my friends were made up of what I like to call *'gifts from nature.'* I treasured the moments I shared talking to the birds and squirrels that often visited my yard for a short visit. As far as I was concerned, they came to see me.

One of my favourite places to visit in those early days was the farm, where I spent many hours under my grandmother's care. Whenever my parents were busy or had to go someplace, they would drop me off at my grandmother's or aunt's farms—spending time at these locations seemed to me as if I had arrived at a large playground with unlimited things to do while making friends with the animals that belonged to either farm. They came in all shapes and sizes, from little chicks, piglets, barn cats and cows, and I would talk, and they would listen. I would follow Gramma when she was busy with her chores, milking the cows, feeding the pigs, or collecting eggs, giving me a chance to chatter away with my animal friends. I was always amazed by her ability to reach right under those chickens sitting on their nests and pull out her hand, holding three eggs at a time. My fondness for chickens was limited, so I never tested it out.

Now, if only I could have as much fun with real friends. I could only imagine having so much fun skipping with someone and running around in a group playing touch-tag or even having a special friend to share my toys with. It seemed a hard lesson to learn that it was not my destiny in those early years to interact much with kids my age before school when there were many kids to get to know. Until that time came, It remained a lonely time, but I learned to be contented with the animals, at least the ones standing still long enough to hear what I had to say.

During my youngest years, on my journey to the farm, I remember looking out the car window and daydreaming about my favourite animal friends. My loneliness would temporarily be set aside as my thoughts were filled with the fun times I would soon be having. However, sometimes, I would catch glimpses of children my age playing in pairs or groups as we drove by. I was unsure if it made me happy or sad, but I envied their merry laughter and smiling faces as they played together. Even in those short drive-by moments, I wondered what it would have been like to have even one human friend my age. Except for that one time when I saw a child sitting down crying and what looked like her playmates laughing at her. I could not imagine what would have caused such a thing to happen. None of my animal friends had ever made me cry, nor could I imagine such a thing happening. I felt pretty smug at that moment as I had only experienced joy while interacting with my special farm friends.

My farm visits would excite me, knowing there would be many things to see and do with my grandmother showing and teaching me all about farming. Then, there was time spent playing in the yard with my favourite animal friend *'Barny.'* I called him that because his usual hangout was at the barn, where I soon realized that cats lived by their wits, catching mice and, of course, could always be found hanging about when the cows were to be milked. They always knew there would be a small bowl of milk for them. You could see at least five or six cats on any given day. Sometimes, I would climb into the hayloft and encounter a batch of kittens. However, I found it strange that no matter how many kittens I would meet in the hopes of having more new friends, there were never more than five or six cats hanging around at milking time. When I was older, I asked my grandmother about the numbers game of the cats, and she helped me better understand the wilder animals that are rarely seen and how it all played out within the survival of the fittest scenario.

Barny was my best cat friend, frequently hanging out with me in the yard by the house, sometimes even joining me while taking a nap on the blanket under the big old shade tree in the summer. There was a rope tied to one of the branches of that tree with a tire tied at the end for swinging, and we would spend many hours swinging back and forth under that lovely tree. It was one of my favourite pastimes with Barny, especially as it was the only time he would let me hold him. Whenever

I turned around on my exploratory journeys around the barnyard, Barny would be close behind. He was a finicky one, but I loved that cat!

When accompanied by my Gramma, I would be busy investigating new and marvellous things and babbling away to the farm animals, no matter their interest in my conversation. I was allowed to interact with most of them once I grew older and better understood their habits. I looked forward to these exploring escapades, except when it came to the chickens. I was not overly fond of those chickens. They did not stay still long enough to listen to what I had to say, nor could you trust what they would do next. Unless you had some food in your hand, they showed little interest whatsoever. I was always nervous around them as they would suddenly fly up close to me, flapping their wings without notification. Thankfully, they seemed to keep their distance whenever Barny was with me.

As an older child, I can look back at my little bubble of happy times and marvel at the life lessons that come, ready or not, leaving no warning time to prepare for what was coming your way. While visiting my aunt when I was around four, I remember finding a small bird while playing in the yard under one of the trees. I was so happy that this little creature let me pick it up and carry it around. I asked my aunt if I could take it with me as we headed to my grandmother's. She agreed that since it was not wounded and figured it had taken its first flying voyage out of the nest, it would be unlikely that the mother bird would come to its rescue. I was thrilled beyond measure to find such a treasure. It was such a precious little thing peeping away in my hand, and I was sure it would be my friend forever.

I was cautious handling the sweet little thing on the car ride with no mournful looks out the window that day. I could hardly wait to show Gramma my prized possession. Jumping out of the car on arrival, I quickly headed to the back door and stopped because my best animal friend, Barny, was waiting for me. My heart was jumping with delight, and I took no notice of my aunt calling and yelling to me, *"Be careful not to..."* as I headed towards the cat. Alas, if only I had heard the rest of her words. I could hardly wait to introduce Barny to my newest friend, the sweet little bird. I did not doubt that he would love this little one as much as me, so how could they not become best friends?

Now you have to remember I was only four and, up until then, did not fully understand all of the habits of animals. I bent down to introduce them, barely getting out the words of introduction, *"Barny, look what I have....,"* which was met with a quick swipe of the paw and into its jaws as it quickly ran away with my prize. What a moment of devastation as I looked around the yard, crying all the while hoping the little one got away. Of course, I never found my tiny bird friend besides a few odd feathers here and there. I am sure that 'Barny' sensed my displeasure as he stayed hidden from me for the rest of the day. Although that dreadful day was unpleasant, the lesson would stay with me forever. Here I was, thinking I was introducing one precious friend to another, offering an exceptional opportunity for friendship.

In hindsight, I can only imagine the thrill my friend 'Barny' felt at being served such a prize!

I have given this lesson much thought over the years and realized that what was learned that day came in many layers regarding friendships, such as things not always being what they seem. Be careful who your friends are because they will not always act as you expect. Trust must be earned. One man's treasure in friendship or things can be seen as entirely different from another perspective. Although some of those lessons took a long time, I eventually grew to be more appreciative of what came my way during this precious journey of life. But I must say the most important lesson of this story… *"one must be wary of cats as they are sly creatures, so be very careful with special friendship offerings!"*

HEALING POWER OF NATURE

"In nature's vast gallery, every step is an opportunity to admire and learn

from the wonders that surround us."

- Gabriel Cruz.

RESTORING ENERGY

"Those who contemplate the beauty of the earth find reserves of strength that will endure as long as life lasts. There is something infinitely healing in the repeated refrains of nature – the assurance that dawn comes after night, and spring after winter."

- Rachel Carson

There was a time when life as I knew it had me stuck in a well of grief and sadness. During that period, strong doubts about ever returning to any sense of 'normality' filled my heart and mind while dealing with three significant deaths over a short period. I recall feeling completely drained and filled with a deep melancholy that seemed to be building versus lessening as the days flew by. This deep remorse began with my loving partner's passing and was reinforced as a way of being a few years later by the consecutive loss of my dearly beloved daughter, followed within a few weeks by my sweet brother's passing. Although immersed in staying strong throughout gatherings of all those left to grieve and despite being filled with gratitude for all the love and support offered, the ache I felt deep in my heart was beginning to take root. My heart was broken despite the knowledge that my loved ones were now free from physical pain, and their energies now reside at a place filled with the kind of peace that passes all understanding.

One of my ways of coping was to recall and talk about times shared with family during moments of mutual love and laughter. What I experienced with these special people in my life journey made it easier to celebrate their lives while holding on tight to an unwavering appreciation for having experienced the connection each held within my heart and the hearts and minds of others. Although I could laugh recalling the many good times and experiences I shared, I wondered how to continue life with the void they left behind. How was it that my world could continue without them? It felt as though my laughter, in some strange way, became a different way of crying because no matter the topic or issue being discussed, a deep sadness remained, leaving me to wonder if I would ever feel normal again. I could not fathom how this deep sadness could ever dissipate or if it would just become a permanent part of the emptiness I was feeling.

I found myself in a complete change of scenery, leaving all that was familiar to spend time with loved ones who were connected to the profound loss of my brother. I spent almost a week in Georgia, where he had lived, followed by a couple of months in Florida with a dear friend and family member in the hopes of finding peace from the turmoil faced over the last few months. It would be a place where even the climate differed from my everyday life routine in Canada. This type of change of everything familiar would relieve the pain. It did not take too long, at least for the most part, before my sadness was replaced with a focus on someone else, including catching up on the lives and loves of close relatives. A new routine was set in motion between visiting, relaxing in a lovely environment, planning little outings to explore some of what was offered in this sunshiny state, and getting accustomed to walking a little dog named Rosie, who never ceased to amaze me with her shenanigans. Luckily for me this sweet little creature filled me with amazement as she seemed to never tire of my babbling during our walks, no matter the subject. Once again one of nature's small creatures brought comfort to my soul.

During this healing time, something extraordinary happened to me during a day's outing to Busch Gardens. It started with just stepping off the tram to the park's front entrance. It was as if a door opened to a more profound sense of pleasure than I had felt for quite some time. It didn't matter if it was for a short or long period. It gave me a sense that nothing is forever. As I passed through the gates, it seemed that the intensity and depth of sadness I felt was lifted off my shoulders. I literally began to feel an uplifted spirit as my steps lightened with the energy of the place we were about to enter. The park's theme at the time, so close to Christmas, brought even more pleasure just viewing the decorations and untold numbers of lights, adding to the ambiance of lightheartedness that I was beginning to feel deep within.

This cheerfulness continued to bloom despite the physical difficulty I was experiencing while walking around the grounds of such a spectacular place. It was fast becoming challenging as this old body was not up to snuff. Strangely enough, while getting from one place to another, I found myself envying folks in wheelchairs, scooters and even strollers. There was a moment or two when I would have gladly traded places with some young kids in little stroller carts being pushed about by their parents. However, to my utter amazement, each of our stops uplifted my spirit more and more making the physical struggles I was facing fade slowly to the background. Unsurprisingly, it turns out that Nature once more came to the rescue.

The first full-hearted and real joy-filled breakthrough for me was the Bird Sanctuary. It was like walking into another dimension while entering the sanctuary. We were greeted by a lush garden of greenery and small trees, including a pond filled with waterfowl of various kinds.

    This nature-filled atmosphere heightened my interest, calling me to watch and listen carefully. The scenery captured my heart, and while I was engrossed in taking pictures of the ducks, a strange sound began to fill the air. It was the sound of a Kookaburra bird. Soon, the air was filled with laughter of many kinds. It was made up of a joyful noise from the mix of humans and birds. These magnificent birds brought about so much light and laughter to all who were within hearing distance. The strange call of the Kookaburra as they communicated with each other is a wonder to behold. I was reminded of the song, *'Kookaburra sits in the old gum tree, merry, merry, merry, merry life has he, laugh Kookaburra, laugh Kookaburra, gay your life must be, ha ha ha.'* Hearing the uniqueness of sound and looking at a Kookaburra bird in a tree affected me so much that I started to sing the song, all the while laughing in mind and heart with the beat of such a rare sound.

INTERLUDES WITH NATURE

Just as it turned out to be a magical moment for me, I doubted anyone listening could refrain from being amused by such hearty sounds of laughter heard throughout the trees near that entrance. It could easily be detected in the faces and laughter heard from others who had just stepped into the sanctuary. I cannot speak for them, but I felt as if I stepped into the garden of Eden as I opened my imagination to fully appreciate all my surroundings. How delightful it became walking through such a lovely sanctuary filled with the sights and various sounds of many other birds. Watching so many species of waterfowl paddling around in little ponds throughout the walk was truly magical. My heart could only sing out, *'Thank you so much, dear Kookaburras*, for the injection of joy during this particular interlude with nature visit. There was now no doubt that laughter certainly holds healing powers beyond expectation.

The next stop only strengthened my heart as it filled up even more with glee observing one of nature's brightest colours of orange flamingoes. I was so surprised to see this colour, reminding me of the Chakra energy as a source of pleasure. It certainly was a pleasing sight. Previously, I had always thought these birds were pink but to my amazement, I learned they come in various colours throughout the spectrum of orange and pink. I was happy that I could capture a few photos of this magnificent colour.

This park, a unique haven, was teeming with a diverse array of so many creatures of nature, a sight rarely seen in this hemisphere and certainly not in my local area. The juxtaposition of this rarity with the human-centric amusements like rides, food, and special shows, only served to heighten the joy welling up within me. No matter which path you choose, there's always a marvel to behold.

During our stroll, we stumbled upon a spacious enclosure for penguins. This expansive land and water habitat, extending right up to our walking path, offered a close-up view of these fascinating creatures. As they gracefully swam in the water, I couldn't help but admire the thoughtful design of the enclosure, which allowed them to approach or retreat from the inquisitive human visitors at their leisure.

A magnificent ride on a slow train passing by open fields filled with various animals and small streams throughout the park was a pure delight. Viewing what would represent the most natural habitat, especially for each animal species, filled my mind with wonder and awe. Having this type of observation of nature only added to my enjoyment. Even though they were too far away to get natural close-up shots for my photo collection, I was happy for them. I was impressed with what my fellow humans had achieved to make the animals more comfortable while being surrounded by a much larger habitat of beings who come to view them. They would raise their heads as the passing train whistle blew, leaving me to ponder if they were content with the efforts made, not being forced to be up close to prying eyes, and I wondered if they, too, felt the same way about who was viewing whom.

My favourite animal stop was the elephant's sanctuary. For some unknown reason, my heart went out to them, wondering how they felt about being there not for their enjoyment, but for the enjoyment of humans. I was happy to capture a few photos of them in their enclosure. They are such magnificent creatures that, although nice to see, I sensed a sad energy from having so little of their natural habitat to move freely about and unable to follow their natural life path. We can only trust that, in some way, the destiny of being captured and penned in, no matter how large the enclosures may be, is not an altogether unpleasant experience for them. Mostly, they seemed at ease or, at worst, bored with the idea of being on display. It can only be hoped that being of service and watched so closely by enthralled humans because of their size and gentleness brings honour to them despite our stares. After all, they are such magnificent creatures.

With heart and mind now brimming to the extent of overflowing with glee, we were able to take in three special Christmas shows during this Busch Gardens excursion. The first was a magic show, followed by a trio acting and singing of the three wise men, and a magnificent ice show to top off the enchanting experience. They all certainly made the problematic walk more than worthwhile, and I had become so enthralled with the entertainment performances that I did not take a single photo. All I could do was sit and take in each magical moment they offered. I could hardly believe the appeal of such a thrilling magic show as I tried to figure out how such feats could take place. I could only look in amazement at the allusion presented. The mystery of it all made me think of how much of life we are unaware of. We as humans spend so much time being caught up with our everyday energy-depleting survival living, keeping us in the dark about the wonder and awe available during our journey. So much of our life experience is magical, and we often miss it.

FINDING A WAY

Reece's Story of Connection

This witness to a fascinating human and animal 'interconnection' is offered to reinforce the depth of understanding possible from one species to another. The interaction began during a trip that took place with my sister-in-law during a scheduled meeting at a highway stop in Florida when I was bringing some of my daughter's ashes to be passed on to one of my daughter's closest friends to distribute, as discussed and planned between them before her death. Since this friend could not meet us to receive the package, she sent her son Jonathan, who lived not far from the designated area, for the exchange. On arrival sat outside of the diner holding a sign, 'Cara's Mother" to make sure he would know who I was. While waiting for his arrival, I noticed a man and young girl walking towards the front entrance accompanied by a large dog harnessed like a service dog giving the impression that there was more to the pet than meets the eye.

    To my surprise, the young man was Jonathan arriving with his daughter, Reese and her pet dog named Elliott. It soon became apparent that the dog was indeed a working dog with complete attention to the young girl giving no notice to the comings and goings of us or others on our way into the building and into the dinning area. I was enthralled by the calmness of the dog walking so close to her and as we sat down, I noticed that the animal immediately lay down behind her chair with no command.

After a short time with the preliminaries of conversation over and after her father explained the unique interconnection of his daughter's 'support' dog, the conversation turned to what I was writing about and I asked for permission to perhaps write about the special connection that we were witnessing. The young girl Reese took a special interest in the conversation about the connection of all nature and began to speak to us of her exceptional understanding of the smallest creatures of this planet, that of bugs. During our lunch experience, she took great pains explaining her unprecedented knowledge of insects, far beyond what the average person would have known. I found her understanding and none stop talking about the topic very interesting as it seemed to me that such an interest at such a young age was beyond imagination and, at the same time, befitting considering my interest in ants that took place when I was about the same age.

How uncanny to hear her talk so proficiently about the world of insects, considering that her father had just explained she suffered from 'social anxiety' that overtly stopped her from interacting with others. He went on to explain that her anxiety level was so high that, in the past at school, she had gone into a seizure just from the thoughts of having to speak to others. It was fascinating to find out that after that incident, they decided to connect her to a pet specifically trained to be an emotional companion with the added bonus of having the ability to sense her level of anxiety. It was further explained that the dog specialized in identifying early signs of unease with her emotional levels and, through specific movements, alerted her by rubbing up against her, allowing her to become more aware before it was too late for her to calm down.

He was very pleased with his daughter's 'comfort level' during our meeting as she had no problems talking about her favourite subject, the world of insects. The level of relaxation of conversation was due to the unique interconnection of the two, especially having the dog continually at her side. It was an exceptional connection that would help Reece avoid entering seizure mode, no matter the situation. The dog's connection to any change in her energy vibration immediately warns her by nudging her to take notice. She can then use a breathing technique to help slow her blood pressure and calm her nerves. Due to this incredible interaction between the two, life has improved to such an extent that Reese could partake in more of the everyday activities with her peers, although Reece remains shy, displaying challenges in social interaction parents no longer must worry every time she is out of sight.

This wonderful dog was, from all accounts, a working dog, trained from a puppy, whose work started as soon as it stepped into a working harness. Jonathan explained that once the harness was removed on entry to their home, the animal completely relaxed into becoming the family pet. Elliott's demeanour would revert to the usual type of performance like most pets, looking for affection and wanting to play, yet no matter the family situation, the dog would stay close to Reese. They were bonded to such a degree that even when she travelled to go and see her grandmother by plane, the animal would accompany her.

Having witnessed folks with 'emotional support animals,' in different settings, and having wondered how it all worked, it is a beautiful thing to not only witness but also discuss with someone who has firsthand knowledge of how it all works. Learning of the special bond created between the two boggles the mind, leaving one to ponder how such a can occur between human and animal natures, and I can only conclude that such interconnections will always remain a mystery.

We all left together after our lunch meeting, and once again, we witnessed the dog's fantastic display of composure, ignoring everyone and staying very close to Reese as we headed out towards the parking lot. On saying our goodbyes, Reese turned to the dog and said, "It's *okay to make friends*," immediately, the dog turned its attention to us, allowing us to pet her dog Elliott's head. To our amazement, the moment was truly magical and we noticed that with but one hardly noticeable tug on the harness, the dog was back to working mode. We said our goodbyes and headed to our car with heads filled with wonder and awe at what had been witnessed on that extraordinary day.

I can only imagine the emotional thoughts of our little group, especially considering the reason to meet in the first place. One can only wonder how through it all this marvelous 'working pet' could not only move through the highs and lows of the emotional levels of energy that was surely present and surrounding us all but have such a miraculous capability to stay in direct connection to its ward and master. How fortunate for Reese that just such a way was found. This depth of ability, at least to my understanding, is a rare thing, surpassing so much of our typical understanding of the human-pet bond leaving room to keep that magic spell of nature and interconnections with all species alive and well.

A CARDINAL'S CALL

*A special interlude with nature that carries
a specific message of benefit to all.*

*The story is based on a Facebook
post by Timothy Mineau*

It is well understood that healing comes in many forms and in many ways for both physical and emotional suffering often experienced in one's life journey. Sometimes just reading about another's experience is enough to bring tears to our eyes as well as move us to a different place of understanding as it resonates with our lives as we contemplate the possibility of a lesson or perhaps even a personal message from what took place. This is one of those stories that speaks to the heart bringing hope and inspiration for all that can be learned from such a simple act of kindness. Healing energy blossoms from the actions of each participant involved. A truly win/win situation all around. A special thanks goes out to Timothy Mineau who took the time to share his excellent and timely interlude with nature through his connection with social media.

According to the post there was an unmistakable lesson to be had from this extraordinary experience that touched Timothy in such a way that he felt inspired to share it with others. The depth of what he received from the experience was enough to encourage him to post for the first time about the incident. It certainly would be considered an unusual interlude with nature at many levels, leaving one to even consider it a *'healing message,'* evidenced from the responses in the comments that followed his post.

His post explained that last October 6th, Timothy arose from a very restless night. It was one of those kinds of nights where sleep eludes due to not sleeping well and having had a lot on his mind and heart at the time. The interlude with nature began while taking 'Mason' to school. As he was pulling out to go down his street, he noticed something explained by him as *"this little guy,"* a small bird on the road. He does not say why but felt the necessity to pull to the side, thinking it would fly away as the car approached. This gesture alone explains a lot the caring nature of this human that was about to experience what most of us only hear about in books, articles or in the movies. In other words, occurrences of this nature are rare.

He goes on to explain that as he slowly drove by, he noticed the small creature did not move. Now Timothy did not say if it was on his way to or from his initial errand where after looking from his side view mirror, he became aware that the bird was still in the same spot. No matter, it was at this time that Timothy pulled his car over, got out and started walking towards the little bird. He found it surprising that as he walked towards the bird having the expectation of it flying away or, at the very least to start struggling to get away, that there was no movement of any kind. You can imagine his surprise and dismay as he was able to walk straight up to it with no signs of distress, allowing him to bend down and pick him up. Timothy recognized by the colour that the bird was a Cardinal. Based on what took place next, you could say this bird was indeed calling out to his heart!

Luckily for all who are privileged to read the tale and see the Facebook post could identify the uniqueness of the situation as shown in the pictures below. How fortunate that Timothy was able to take a couple of pictures having with his phone camara close at hand.

Timothy found that he did not have to restrain him in anyway while examining him and finding no identifying signs of injury, as seen in the pictures he provided in his post. Due to the strangeness of it all with such an unusual reaction from his close proximity to the bird, and despite not finding any kind of injuries, Timothy had no doubt that something was not right. Now this is the point where most of us become awed and moved by the uniqueness of the experience realizing, like Timothy, there is a deeper meaning to what is happening. Almost as if the bird is willing him to pick him up you might even say.

Due to the uncommon reaction of the bird, Timothy pulled him close to his heart and began to pet him gently. He decided that he would take him to the CNC, a place that offers help for wildlife. It would be a couple of hours before they opened so Timothy continued to hold him, recognizing that for some uncanny reason he sensed an immediate bond. This bond became obvious as the bird looked him right in the eye and put his beak to his nose. After a bit of time had passed, he was finally able to take the '*little guy*' to CNC. Unfortunately, for this little creature, they do not take songbirds. Only birds of prey are taken in for treatment. However, they were kind enough to examine him and provide Timothy with an alternative solution for the small creature.

Upon examination, they determined he had broken his clavicle, further explaining that, just like humans, it is excruciating for birds. It was thought that the little bird was more than likely hit by a car. They recommended a place for Timothy to take him, located in a spot which he determined would take a little over an hour one way with traffic. This left him wondering how he would manage as he had a full day ahead of him and did not know how to make it work. At this point, Timothy was unsure of what to do. He stated in his post that as he sat in the car trying to decide what he would do, the little bird began to sing. Astonished due to the type of injury this poor little creature had to endure, and after hearing such a sound, Timothy's thought process changed direction. This change in priorities took place while looking down at the little box he had placed him in, and in doing so, he found the bird was looking up at him. One can only marvel at the possibility that this little bird was also wondering what he would do.

Enraptured with what was happening, the 'little guy' continued to look up while letting out a couple more little notes, and tears began to fill Timothy's eyes. How could it be? Here he sat with this tiny little creature experiencing a great deal of pain, suffering with a broken clavicle, and yet, he still sang. Timothy explained that he sat there for a few minutes just looking at him. He reached over and gave him a gentle stroke on his head and said, thank you, little guy. It is easy to see that just from observing such a gesture from one of nature's tiny creatures, Timothy seemed to have only one decision to make, a selfless action that, I might add, was a noble act of kindness!

There was no more hesitation as Timothy called in to work, asking that all of his meetings for the day be rescheduled. He went on to explain that he called the recommended songbird place for some help, and a wonderful human named Nancy told him to bring the little bird in. The now two separate species of life sped off on a journey to a different location for special treatment. Although separated species, they undoubtedly were connected in such a way that it is difficult to measure.

On arrival, Nancy examined the Cardinal and confirmed that the little bird had a broken clavicle but that its air sacs were full of fluid as well and needed to be released for any type of healing to take place. She explained the process, relaying that there would be a three—to four-week recovery ahead for the Cardinal. Timothy also learned that after such a procedure, some birds make it, and some do not because of the uncertainty of what may happen internally due to being hit by a car.

Timothy was informed that if the bird fully recovers, it will need to be released where it was found. Cardinals generally have a family. Over the recovery time, this poor little creature had a rough road after learning that there were a couple of times Nancy wasn't sure he would make it, as he stopped eating a few times and without nourishment, there would not be enough healing energy to recover. What a relief that he pushed through. Timothy was thrilled with the prospect of picking him up after a full recovery and releasing him back into his natural habitat, the world of nature.

In his exact words, Timothy states,

> *"I share this experience with you because this little bird reminded me that we can still sing even when we are struggling. When we are struggling and in pain, we can still make a difference. He reminded me that every living thing is significant, no matter what. If it has life, it deserves*

love. It is a birthright! He reminded me to stop, take it slow, and always, ALWAYS, let love lead. On a day when I was struggling with some pretty heavy things, he reminded me to… sing!"

Story Reflection

Sharing this particular story brings about a strong awareness of the uniqueness of connection available with all creatures found on this beautiful planet no matter their size.

How marvelous that so often much needed healing arrives much like the phrase, 'healing comes in mysterious ways, it's wonders to perform,' and that no matter the circumstances, nature speaks eternally to our hears and minds as we open ourselves to what is so lovingly offered throughout this life journey experience.

CONCLUSION

As I reflect over the many years of life through personal observations as well as hearing intriguing stories about nature from others, I have found that in some form or another, there is a strong urge to reconnect. Every time I feel that tug at my heart something happens to bring me to a higher state of joy. With every opportunity that comes, another of nature's mysteries opens itself up for exploration. No matter what form that connection takes, when crossing my path, I find myself in complete harmony with my surroundings.

Each time my mind revisits my encounters from the past, I am left with more food for thought, expanding understanding and leaving new avenues to rethink the mysteries I find in my life. Thus far, nature has given me more than a sense of belief in something bigger than previously understood. These encounters opened my heart and mind to an uncanny knowing something more about the creative force that gives us life, leaving no doubts that all creation is connected and that we, as humans, are privileged to experience this physical life as a gift from this beautiful planet. It has been and continues to be a most pleasurable 'earthly visit' with untold moments of wonder and awe within the abundance of nature that surrounds us all.

I truly believe that we hold within our grasp the keys to a better understanding of Love, Light and Energy offered as a gift through the unique opportunities we encounter throughout this earthly experience, especially if we remain open and receptive to what the world of nature has to offer. It has been a privilege to share some of the magic, wonder and emotional healing experienced through these stories that hopefully they will capture your heart and mind just as they did those of us who were willing to share our interludes with nature. I hope you, the reader, will find as much joy and pleasure in these stories as I, the author, have found in compiling them for your reading pleasure.

The End

For more information,
feel free to visit the author's website at:
www.carolynnmccully.com

www.ingramcontent.com/pod-product-compliance
Lightning Source LLC
Chambersburg PA
CBHW052029030426
42337CB00027B/4929